MEN WE

REAPED

MEN WE REAPED

A MEMOIR

JESMYN WARD

BLOOMSBURY

New York · London · New Delhi · Sydney

Some of the names, locations, and details of events in this book have been changed to protect the privacy of people involved.

Published by Bloomsbury USA, New York

All papers used by Bloomsbury USA are natural, recyclable products made from wood grown in well-managed forests. The manufacturing processes conform to the environmental regulations of the country of origin.

LIBRARY OF CONGRESS CATALOGING-IN-PUBLICATION DATA
Ward, Jesmyn.
    Men we reaped : a memoir / Jesmyn Ward.—First U.S. edition.
        pages cm
    Includes bibliographical references and index.
    ISBN 978-1-60819-521-3 (alk. paper)
    1. Ward, Jesmyn.   2. African American women authors—Biography.   3. Rural poor—Mississippi—Biography.
4. African American men—Mississippi.   I. Title.
    PS3623.A7323Z46 2013
    813'.6—dc23
    [B]

                                              2013013600

First U.S. edition 2013

1   3   5   7   9   10   8   6   4   2

Typeset by Westchester Book Group
Printed and bound in the U.S.A. by Thomson-Shore Inc., Dexter, Michigan

FOR JOSHUA ADAM DEDEAUX,
WHO LEADS WHILE I FOLLOW

We saw the lightning and that was the guns; and then we heard the thunder and that was the big guns; and then we heard the rain falling and that was the blood falling; and when we came to get in the crops, it was dead men that we reaped.
—Harriet Tubman

Young adolescents in our prime live a life of crime,
Though it ain't logical, we hobble through these trying
    times.
Living blind: Lord, help me with my troubled soul.
Why all my homies had to die before they got to grow?
—from "Words 2 My Firstborn," Tupac Shakur

I stand on the stump
of a child, whether myself
or my little brother who died, and
yell as far as I can, I cannot leave this place, for
for me it is the dearest and the worst,
it is life nearest to life which is
life lost: it is my place where
I must stand. . . .
—from "Easter Morning," A. R. Ammons

CONTENTS

PROLOGUE

Whenever my mother drove us from coastal Mississippi to New Orleans to visit my father on the weekend, she would say, "Lock the doors." After my mother and father split for the last time before they divorced, my father moved to New Orleans, while we remained in DeLisle, Mississippi. My father's first house in the Crescent City was a modest one-bedroom, painted yellow, with bars on the window. It was in Shrewsbury, a small Black neighborhood that spread under and to the north of the causeway overpass. The house was bounded by a fenced industrial yard to the north and by the rushing, plunking sound of the cars on the elevated interstate to the south. I was the oldest of four, and since I was the oldest, I was the one who bossed my one brother, Joshua, and my two sisters, Nerissa and Charine, and my cousin Aldon, who lived with us for years, to arrange my father's extra sheets and sofa cushion into pallets on the living room floor so we all had enough room to sleep. My parents, who were attempting to reconcile and would fail, slept in the only bedroom. Joshua insisted that there was a ghost in the house, and at night we'd lie on our backs in the TV-less living room, watch the barred shadows slink across the walls, and wait for something to change, for something that wasn't supposed to be there, to move.

"Somebody died here," Josh said.

"How you know?" I said.

"Daddy told me," he said.

"You just trying to scare us," I said. What I didn't say: *It's working.*

I was in junior high then, in the late eighties and early nineties, and I attended a majority White, Episcopalian Mississippi private school. I was a small-town girl, and my classmates in Mississippi were as provincial as I was. My classmates called New Orleans the "murder capital." They told horror stories about White people being shot while unloading groceries from their cars. Gang initiations, they said. What was unspoken in this conversation—and, given the racist proclivities of more than a few of my classmates, I'm surprised that it was unspoken—was that these gangsters, ruthlessly violent and untethered by common human decency, were Black. My school peers would often glance at me when they spoke about Black people. I was a scholarship kid, only attending the school because my mother was a maid for a few wealthy families on the Mississippi coast who sponsored my tuition. For most of my junior high and high school years, I was the only Black girl in the school. Whenever my classmates spoke about Black people or New Orleans and tried to not look at me but inevitably did, I stared back at them and thought about the young men I knew from New Orleans, my father's half brothers.

Uncle Bookie was our favorite of my father's half brothers. He and his brothers had spent their lives in the neighborhoods my classmates most feared. Uncle Bookie looked the most like the grandfather I'd barely known, who'd died of a stroke at age fifty. He had a chest like a barrel, and his eyes closed when he smiled. On hot days, Uncle Bookie would walk us through Shrewsbury toward the highway in the sky, to a ramshackle shotgun house, maroon in my memory, that stood on the corner. The lady who lived in the house sold ice pops out of the back. They were liquid sugar, and melted too quickly in the heat. On the walk to her yard, he'd crack jokes, gather more kids, lead us over the melting asphalt like a hood pied piper. Once our ice pops melted to syrup in their cardboard cups, once Joshua and I had licked the sugar water from our hands and arms, Uncle Bookie would play games with us in the street: kickball, football, and basketball. He laughed when the football hit one of us in the mouth, leaving it sore and swollen, his eyes slit to the thin side of a penny. On some days he would take us with our father and his pit bull to the park under the highway. There, my father fought his dog against other dogs. The other men who watched or coaxed their dogs to savagery were dark and sweat-glazed as their animals in the heat. My brother and I always stood close to our uncle. We grabbed his forearms, holding tightly, flinching as the cars boomed overhead and the animals ripped at each other. Afterward, the dogs panted and smiled while they bled, and my brother and I relaxed our grip on our uncle, and were happy to leave the shadowed world and the threat of a dog lunging outside the fighting circle.

"Daddy ain't tell you no story about nobody dying in here," I said.

"Yeah, he did," Joshua said.

"You telling it," Aldon said.

When I was in high school, I could not reconcile the myth

of New Orleans to the reality, but I knew that there was truth somewhere. My father and mother sat in the front seat of the car during those early nineties visits, when they were still married but separated, when they still had the easy rapport that years of marriage engenders, and they talked about shootings, about beatings, about murder. They gave the violence of New Orleans many names. We never saw any of that when we visited my father. But we listened to the chain-link fence rattle in the industrial yard next to my father's house and the night stretched on interminably, and we listened to my brother tell us ghost stories.

Yet we knew another New Orleans existed. We saw that when we piled into my mother's car and rode past the red brick projects scattered through New Orleans, two-story buildings with sagging iron balconies, massive old trees standing like sentinels at each side of the buildings, women gesticulating and scratching their heads, small dark children playing angrily, happily, sulking on the broken sidewalks. I eyed the young men through the car window. Men in sagging pants with their heads bent together, murmuring, ducking into corner stores that sold POBOYS SHRIMP OYSTER. I wondered what the men were talking about. I wondered who they were. I wondered what their lives were like. I wondered if they were murderers. At night on my father's living room floor, I asked Joshua again.

"What Daddy say happen?" I said.

"Said somebody got shot," Joshua said.

"What somebody?"

"A man," he said to the ceiling. Charine burrowed into my side.

"Shut up," Nerissa said. Aldon sighed.

When we left my father to go home to DeLisle, as we did every Sunday, I was sad. We all were sad, I think, even my mother, who was trying to make their marriage work, despite the distance and the years of infidelity. She'd even been contemplating moving to New Orleans, a city she hated. I missed my father. I didn't want to return to school in Mississippi on Monday morning, to walk through the glass doors to the large, fluorescent-lit classrooms, the old desks, my classmates perched on the backs of them, wearing collared shirts and khaki shorts, their legs spread, their eyeliner blue. I didn't want them to look at me after saying something about Black people, didn't want to have to avert my eyes so they didn't see me studying them, studying the entitlement they wore like another piece of clothing. Our drive home took us through New Orleans East, across the Isle Sauvage bayou, over the gray murmur of Lake Pontchartrain, through the billboards and strip malls of Slidell into Mississippi. We took I-10 past the pine wall of Stennis Space Center, past Bay St. Louis, past Diamondhead to DeLisle. Once there, we would have exited the long, pitted highway, driven past Du Pont, shielded like Stennis behind its wall of pine trees, past the railroad tracks, past the small wooden houses set in small fields and small sandy yards, trees setting the porches in shade. Here horses stood still in fields, munching grass, seeking cool. Goats chewed fence posts.

DeLisle and Pass Christian, the two towns where all of my family hails from, are not New Orleans. Pass Christian squats beside the man-made beach of the Gulf of Mexico alongside Long Beach, the Bay of St. Louis at its back, while

DeLisle hugs the back of the Bay of St. Louis before spreading away and thinning further upcountry. The streets of both towns are sleepy through much of the barely bearable summer, and through much of the winter, when temperatures hover near freezing. In DeLisle during the summers, there are sometimes crowds on Sundays at the county park because younger people come out to play basketball and play music from their cars. In the spring, the older people gather at the local baseball field, where Negro leagues from throughout the South come to play. On Halloween, children still walk or ride on the backs of pickup trucks through the neighborhood from house to house to trick-or-treat. On All Saints Day, families gather around loved ones' graves, bring nylon and canvas folding chairs to sit in after they've cleaned headstones and sandy plots, arranged potted mums, and shared food. They talk into the evening, burn fires, wave away the last of the fall gnats. This is not a murder capital.

Most of the Black families in DeLisle have lived there as far back as they can remember, including mine, in houses many of them built themselves. These houses, small shotguns and A-frames, were built in waves, the oldest in the thirties by our great-grandparents, the next in the fifties by our grandparents, the next in the seventies and eighties by our parents, who used contractors. These modest houses, ours included, had two to three bedrooms with gravel and dirt driveways and rabbit hutches and scupadine vineyards in the back. Poor and working-class, but proud. There is no public housing at all in DeLisle, and the project housing that existed before Hurricane Katrina in Pass Christian consisted of several small redbrick duplexes and a few subdivisions with single-family homes, which housed some Black people, some Vietnamese. Now, seven years after Katrina, developers build two- and three-bedroom houses up on fifteen- to twenty-foot stilts where this public housing stood, and these houses fill quickly with those still displaced from the storm, or young adults from Pass Christian and DeLisle who want to live in their hometown. Hurricane Katrina made that impossible for several years, since it razed most of the housing in Pass Christian, and decimated what was closest to the bayou in DeLisle. Coming home to DeLisle as an adult has been harder for this reason, a concrete one. And then there are abstract reasons, too.

As Joshua said when we were kids hunting down ghosts: *Somebody died here.*

From 2000 to 2004, five Black young men I grew up with died, all violently, in seemingly unrelated deaths. The first was my brother, Joshua, in October 2000. The second was Ronald in December 2002. The third was C. J. in January 2004. The fourth was Demond in February 2004. The last was Roger in June 2004. That's a brutal list, in its immediacy and its relentlessness, and it's a list that silences people. It silenced me for a long time. To say this is difficult is understatement; telling this story is the hardest thing I've ever done. But my ghosts were once people, and I cannot forget that. I cannot forget that when I am walking the streets of DeLisle, streets that seem even barer since Katrina. Streets that seem even more empty since all these deaths, where instead of hearing my friends or my brother playing music from their cars at the county park, the only sound I hear is a tortured parrot that one of my cousins owns, a parrot that screams so loudly it sounds through the neighborhood, a scream like a wounded child, from a cage so small the parrot's crest barely clears the top of the cage while its tail brushes the bottom. Sometimes when that parrot screams, sounding its rage and grief, I wonder at my neighborhood's silence. I wonder why silence is the sound of our subsumed rage, our accumulated grief. I decide this is not right, that I must give voice to this story.

I'm telling you: there's a ghost in here, Joshua said.

Because this is my story just as it is the story of those lost young men, and because this is my family's story just as it is my community's story, it is not straightforward. To tell it, I must tell the story of my town, and the history of my community. And then I must revisit each of the five young black men who died: follow them backward in time, from Rog's death to Demond's death to C. J.'s death to Ronald's death to my brother's death. At the same time, I must tell this story forward through time, so between those chapters where my friends and my brother live and speak and breathe again for a few paltry pages, I must write about my family and how I grew up. My hope is that learning something about our lives and the lives of the people in my community will mean that when I get to the heart, when my marches forward through the past and backward from the present meet in the middle with my brother's death, I'll understand a bit better why this epidemic happened, about how the history of racism and economic inequality and lapsed public and personal responsibility festered and turned sour and spread here. Hopefully, I'll understand why my brother died while I live, and why I've been saddled with this rotten fucking story.

WE ARE IN WOLF TOWN
DISTANT PAST–1977

In pictures, some of my ancestors on my mother's and my father's sides are so light-skinned as to look white, and some are so dark the lines of the nose, a mouth, look silver in the black and white picture. They wear long-sleeved, full white shirts tucked into dark skirts, and muted cotton shirts tucked into loose pants. Inevitably, they stand outside in these pictures, but the backgrounds are so faded, one can only see trees like smoke behind them. None of them smile. My grandmother Dorothy tells me stories about them, says some of them were Haitian, that others were Choctaw, said they spoke French, that they came from New Orleans or a nebulous elsewhere, searching for land and space, and they stopped here.

Before DeLisle was named DeLisle, after a French settler, the early settlers called it Wolf Town. Pine and oak and sweetgum grow in tangles from the north down to the south of the town, to the DeLisle Bayou. The Wolf River, brown and lazy, snakes its way through DeLisle, fingers the country in creeks, before emptying into the bayou. When people ask me about my hometown, I tell them it was called after a wolf before it was partially tamed and settled. I want to impart something of its wild roots, its early savagery. Calling it Wolf Town hints at the wildness at the heart of it.

I want to tell them, but don't: *I've seen foxes, small and red and thin-boned, darting along ditches before slipping into woods again. This thing that I saw once was different. It was night, and my friends and I were riding through a part of DeLisle that had been previously untouched, a wild tangle of wood that someone had cut a dead-end road into in hopes of building a subdivision. The creature loped out of the woods before us, and we startled and shouted, and it looked at us and loped back into the darkness, and it was darkness, colored black, and had a long, fine snout, and it was soundless, this wild thing that looked at us like the intruders that we were before we drove away from it to more well-traveled roads, away from that place that was everything but dead end, that place that seemed all beginning, a birthplace: Wolf Town.*

But I am not that eloquent, so I shut my mouth and smile.

MOST OF THE people here are kin. It is something that the "Black" people will talk about among themselves, the way our families intertwine and feed one another, and it is something that "White" people will speak about among themselves, but it is something that we rarely speak to each other about, even when those on both sides of the color divide share the same last name. We are conscious of the way bloodlines are so entangled in our community, so much so that back in the early 1900s, adults in DeLisle would arrange visits with other communites of mixed-race people in Alabama or Louisiana to match children with marriageable mates to vary the gene pool. Sometimes this worked, and sometimes it didn't. Sometime the matches the young found were closer to home. Sometimes they were cousins, or in other ways had relationships that were taboo.

My maternal grandmother, Dorothy, remembers when she was very young, before her mother, Mary, and father, Harry, had all of their twelve kids, riding in her father's old car to visit relatives farther up in the country, north of DeLisle. Harry's father was a dark, rich brown, but his mother was, by all accounts, White, and her sister lived in a cluster of White communities farther north. Harry's children ranged from cinammon to nutmeg to vanilla, and on that trip north, the children curled in on themselves in the car's rumble seat and rode through the hot bright Mississippi wilderness under blankets. Harry was light enough to be mistaken for White. While there, the children played inside the house, and when the sun began to set, my great-great-grandmother's sister told her, "Well, it's about time for y'all to be getting down the road." What she said without saying was: *It's not safe for you here. The Klan are here. You should not be caught out on these roads in the dark.* So my grandmother and her siblings folded their small bodies in two and hid under the suffocating blanket again, and a seemingly White man and his White mother drove south to DeLisle, to the mostly Creole, mixed-race community they called home.

My mother's paternal grandfather Adam Jr.'s family also bears stories like this. My mother has a picture of Adam Jr.'s father, Adam Sr., and he looks White. In fact, he was half White and half Native American. Adam Sr.'s father was Joseph Dedeaux, a White man, in a family of White Dedeauxes that had some money and owned some of the most beautiful land in DeLisle. The land sits in the curve of the bayou and is graced by almost unbearably grand live oaks. The sun sets over the marsh grass and water, turning it into a tableau so gorgeous it haunts my homesick dreams. This White man fell in love with his Native American housekeeper, and he began a relationship with her. When his family found out, they disowned him. So Joseph married Daisy and bore my great-grandfather. Later, my mother told me that Joseph and Daisy established a general store, where my White great-great-grandfather would die, a victim of a shooting and a botched store robbery. My Native American great-great-grandmother followed him a few years later from illness.

My mother's maternal great-grandfather, Jeremy, also was fairly wealthy. It is rumored that his wife's people came from Haiti but that he was a Native American. When he realized that the White government would do nothing to educate his children and grandchildren, he built a one-room school on the land he owned and hired a teacher. He also spent some of his time out in the woods on his multi-acre property, tending to liquor stills, which was a common pastime in the community during Prohibition. One of those days, he and his son-in-law Harry were working them together, and the Revenues found them. I imagine these White men wearing white shirts and dark pants, their hair lank and sweaty, their guns smooth and cool in their moist hands. Harry ran and escaped, and would later live to hide his children under blankets to take them upcountry to visit their White relatives, but my great-great-grandfather Jeremy was shot and killed. The Revenues left his dead body to grow cold in the green reaching woods among his ruined stills, and once Harry told them what had happened, his family trekked into the forest to retrieve his body.

★　★　★

MY FATHER'S FATHER was called Big Jerry, and Jerry and his siblings and their mother, Ellen, lived across the street from St. Stephen's Church in a small, square house, painted slate blue. My paternal great-grandparents owned a couple of acres along St. Stephen's Road, and when my father was younger, the fields were planted with corn and crops, and there were horses.

My mother's father, Adam Jr., lived in another small house, but this one at the end of an even narrower road that runs parallel to St. Stephen's on the north. There's a slight hill north of St. Stephen's, the kind of gradual incline that can go unnoticed unless one is hauling a load or riding a bike; the road that leads from St. Stephen's and ascends this hill was aptly named Hill Road, and the small road that branches off Hill Road and runs perpendicular, barely wide enough for one car to drive on, is Alpine. My maternal great-grandparents' long and narrow house is at the end of this road, modest and well-kept and gray. This is where my great-grandmother Maman Vest lived.

Both great-grandmothers were olive-complexioned and had white and black salt-pepper hair. Both had thick Creole French accents. I mostly visited Mother Ellen with my father. I never met her husband, my great-grandfather, but my father says he was shot after some sort of argument and died young. Mother Ellen had a loud, strong voice, and she was funny, like my father. She sat whole afternoons on her porch, watching the comings and goings of the neighborhood, and drove well, but slowly, into her old age. When we visited, she sat on the steps of the front porch and told us stories about her youth, when she and her siblings pulled Spanish moss from the oak trees to stuff their mattresses. They were hard workers then, accustomed to long hours weeding and planting and harvesting fields, and caring for livestock. Maman Vest would never sit on a stoop with us: she was a bit more proper, a bit more reserved, but we would all sit in the cool shade of her dark porch, where the children ate cake and listened to the grown-ups gossip. Maman Vest told us stories of her dead husband, Adam Senior, who she said had visited her once after he died as she lay in her bed. He stood, framed in the doorway, and spoke to her. She said she was afraid, that she was paralyzed and could not move. I never met her husband, my great-grandfather Adam Senior, the man or the ghost. Maman often told us stories about him, her dead husband, but never spoke of Aldon, the lost son who died in Vietnam after stepping on a land mine.

Men's bodies litter my family history. The pain of the women they left behind pulls them from the beyond, makes them appear as ghosts. In death, they transcend the circumstances of this place that I love and hate all at once and become supernatural. Sometimes, when I think of all the men who've died early in my family over the generations, I think DeLisle is the wolf.

I LIKE TO think my parents met somewhere in the middle, somewhere in the wide swath of woods that separated their fathers' houses, or perhaps on St. Stephen's Road, which was then hard-packed red dirt. They would have both been barefoot, I think, and it would have been the late fifties. My father would have seen a thin olive-skinned girl with small bones and a narrow nose, her dark brown curly hair smoothed to her head. She would have smiled, and her face, beautifully symmetrical, would have blossomed. She would have been happy to be free for a day with her siblings, free to play. Because my grandmother Dorothy worked so much to support her children, my mother tended to household chores and her younger siblings. My father may not have been able to see her strength then, but it was there. My mother would have seen a boy the color of pecans, his hair darkest black and smoothed straight back from his wide, short forehead, his nose wide and prominent, his cheekbones even then like large rocks in his face. He may have been wearing an eye patch. His older cousin shot him in the left eye with a BB gun by accident when he was six, and the eye shriveled in his face and turned gray. It would be some time before it was removed and a false eye put in its place, so my father spent much of his childhood and teenage years wearing a patch. Like all children, they were the children of history and place, of southern Mississippi and Louisiana, both their family lines mixed with African, French, Spanish, and Native ancestry all smoothed to the defining *Black* in the American South, but even though they would have seen that history bearing fruit in each other, they would not have been thinking about that.

My mother would have been looking at the dead eye in my father's face, maybe seeing that the dry gray marble made the rest of him all the more terribly beautiful, and my father would have looked at my mother's small, slender arms and legs and been reminded of a doe. The pines would have reached up and away on both sides of the road, and my parents would not have said hello when they first met each other. My father would have kicked dirt into the ditch. My mother would have picked up a rock. They knew kids in common, their cousins, and other friends. This was and still is a small town.

In 1969, when my father was thirteen and my mother eleven, Hurricane Camille hit. It flattened everything, wiped away the landscape with an indomitable hand. I imagine everyone in south Mississippi must have thought the world was at an end. Camille was only one in a staccato succession of tragedies in those days. Southern Mississippi boys, Black and White, died in Vietnam, cities all over the United States imploded in riots, and churches were bombed. Crosses burned. Freedom Riders tried to register folks to vote, and in Mississippi, the rivers and bayous were watery graveyards. Locally, Black men and women were demonstrating on public beaches where they were not allowed to sunbathe and swim. In return, they were being attacked by dogs and policemen. They must have thought the end times had come when Hurricane Camille, a Category 5 storm, bore down on them, killing more than 250 people, drowning a family of thirteen who'd searched out shelter in a Catholic church in Pass Christian. The hobbled authorities put families in tent cities. After my grandmother Celestine's house was lifted from its foundation and displaced by the storm surge that leveled Pass Christian, my father and his sisters and mother stayed in one such tent city. My grandmother Dorothy's house was spared, since it sits farther up in DeLisle in a part that we call the Chaneaux, which is distant enough from the DeLisle Bayou to escape the surge. My mother's family provided water for the entire town when people learned that there was an artesian spring in their yard.

After Hurricane Camille hit, the government also offered hurricane survivors the chance to relocate elsewhere. My father's family was given the option of moving from Pass Christian to Oakland, California, so they left. This same trend of relocating those affected by major hurricanes would occur decades later, when Hurricane Katrina ravaged the Mississippi Gulf Coast, and instead of being given the tools they needed to help rebuild home, families were offered one option: relocation. Escape. My father and his mother and siblings fled from the memory of their house rocking off its foundation while they swam to say alive in the attic. In Oakland, the Black Panthers fed him breakfast before school, and during the summers his family drove to Mississippi for visits. For all of us, the pull home is an inexorable thing. During his Mississippi summers, my father hung out with his cousins and extended family, and sometimes, I'm sure, with my mother.

My father grew solid and his pectorals were so well muscled they looked striated like clam shells. In the Bay Area, he took kung fu, and his first master taught him how to fight honestly, mean: *First, punch them in the nose.* Daddy was a natural; when jumped by three hustlers after a three-card monte game gone wrong on a city bus, he beat them all. He joined a gang. He dated plenty of girls: he was handsome and charming and funny, muscular and artistic.

In some ways, both of my parents were given adult responsibility too early, a necessity of growing up in fatherless households. Those shy children they'd been on St. Stephen's when they met had grown and changed in their teenage years. My grandmother Celestine treated my father as the man of the house and the family, as an adult equal, since she'd married and divorced his father, my grandfather Jerry, and was raising her children on her own. For years, my father was the only boy in the house, and he was the second-eldest child. He called my grandmother Celestine "Mama" sometimes, and other times he called her "Lady," and from him it sounded like an endearment, an address of devotion from an equal. This meant he had the freedom to explore Oakland and the Bay Area, to experiment with drugs, to do some petty hustling.

Just as my father was the father figure in his family, the older boy of two and the second-oldest child, my mother was the mother figure in her own family. My mother wasn't accorded the kind of freedom my father was granted because of his gender. Instead, since my grandmother Dorothy worked two or three jobs to support her seven children on her own, since she spent her days working as hard, physically, as any man, the role of mothering the seven children fell to my mother. After several years of marriage, my grandfather Adam divorced my grandmother to marry her friend. So my mother learned to cook before she turned ten, and spent the rest of her preteen and teenage years preparing large breakfasts of oatmeal and biscuits, and larger dinners of red beans and rice. When my four uncles, the youngest of the seven children, broke my grandmother's rules my mother whipped them with switches peeled from trees in the yard.

She and her two sisters washed loads of laundry and hung them out to dry on lines stretched across the length of the swampy backyard.

This set my mother apart from her siblings: she was one of them, and not. The role she assumed made her lonely and isolated her, and her natural shyness complicated this. She resented the strength she had to cultivate, the endurance demanded of women in the rural South. She recognized its injustice, even as a child. This made her quiet and withdrawn. By the time she was a teenager and her siblings old enough to not need her constant supervision, my mother was able to act her age, and she dated, frequented the hole-in-the-wall club her godfather owned, and threw a few house parties that her peers still talk about today.

Still, she felt the confines of gender and the rural South and the seventies stalking her, felt that specter of DeLisle out in the darkness, the wolf cornering her in her mother's house, which had no heat in the winter, no air in the summer. She was relieved when she graduated from high school and traveled to Los Angeles to live with relatives on her father's side to go to school. This was a rare opportunity for her, and even though she was aware of how rare it was, how tenuous, the dream of my father called to her in Oakland. After a semester of study, she headed north to the Bay Area to join my father. He had courted her with letters and pictures sent from Oakland and with charm and muscled beauty when he saw her during the summers he visited Mississippi. This is how they began their lives together.

ROGER ERIC DANIELS III

BORN: MARCH 5, 1981
DIED: JUNE 3, 2004

ANN ARBOR WAS gray. The sky was always overcast, blanched sooty and cold, even though it was spring and the trees had bloomed bright green. I was miserable with allergies. I'd just finished the first year of my two-year graduate program, and my nose was running so badly I could only breathe out of my mouth. I'd never had allergies like that before my time in Michigan, and having them then made me feel as if the very landscape in Michigan hated me, as if I were a foreign body it was attempting to eject.

My cousin Aldon flew into Detroit to help me drive from Michigan to Mississippi for the summer of 2004. Joshua was a month older than Aldon, and we'd grown up as close as siblings. As I was twenty-seven, he had grown into my big cousin at twenty-four, dwarfing me by seven inches. He had a gold tooth, braids cornrowed thickly to his head, and everything about him was capable and kind, so when he took the driver's seat for the first leg of the fifteen-hour drive, I hunched over in the passenger seat, glared at the miles of highway, fields, and billboards before us, and was grateful and apprehensive. *I would like to breathe again*, I thought, but I was going home. My homesickness always meant that the thought of going home was exhilarating and comforting, but over the past four years, that sense of promise had turned to dread. When my brother died in October 2000, it was as if all the tragedy that had haunted my family's life took shape in that great wolf of DeLisle, a wolf of darkness and grief, and that great thing was bent on beating us. By the summer of 2004, three of my friends had died as well: Ronald in the winter of 2002, C. J. in January 2004, and Demond a month later, in February. Each friend's subsequent death was a hard blow, as that wolf hunted us. But I didn't say this to Aldon. Instead, I said: "I can't breathe, cuz. It's the air."

Aldon turned up the music: rap. It beat us down those highways, over the miles. By the time we stopped in the middle of the plain farmland of Ohio for Coke, for bathroom breaks, for snacks, I didn't have to plug my nose with tissue. By the time we crossed the Ohio River over to Kentucky's rolling green hills, I could inhale and exhale through my nose. Aldon drove with his left hand on the wheel, his right on the armrest, centered.

I hope nobody dies this summer, I thought.

WHILE MY CLASSMATES remained in Ann Arbor or worked on fishing boats in Alaska or visited family in Cape Cod during their summer breaks, I always went home to Mississippi. I had done the same every winter break, every spring break, and every summer break while I was an undergrad at Stanford University from 1995 to 2000, and I continued the tradition in the summer of 2004. Homesickness had troubled me ever since I'd left for Stanford in 1995. I would hide weird crying jags from my then-boyfriend when I saw down-on-their-luck men who reminded me of my father. I would beg long conversations on the phone with my friends at home so I could listen to the sounds in the background, wishing I were there. I dreamed of the woods surrounding my mother's house, that they were being razed and burned. I knew there was much to hate about home, the racism and inequality and poverty, which is why I'd left, yet I loved it.

During visits, I lived in my mother's house, a white double-wide trailer, set on the back of an acre, away from the road. Spanish oaks and small garden plots filled with azaleas and bulbs dotted the front yard. My mother was proud of her yard and worked hard at cultivating it, even though we lived at the top of a hill, which meant that when the heavy rains came during the spring and the summer, the earth washed down the hill into the street, and the front part of the yard remained sandy. Joshua was four years dead that summer, so my mother had converted his room into a bedroom for my seven year-old nephew, De'Sean. My middle sister, De'Sean's mother, Nerissa, twenty-one, lived in a duplex apartment in Long Beach, Mississippi, at the time. She'd given birth to De'Sean when she was thirteen, and hadn't had the opportunity or the maturity to be a mother to him, so De'Sean lived with my mother, and Nerissa had learned to mother him on weekends. My youngest sister, Charine, eighteen, still lived in my mom's house. She graduated from high school days after I made it home from Michigan.

When Aldon and I arrived from our long drive, I let myself

in the back door, tiptoed into Charine's room, and climbed into bed with her. She didn't turn me away, even though I was sweating Coke and Corn Nuts with concentration thinned to its most desperate. I threw an arm around her, faced her back. We were the same height, nearly the same weight, had the same long-limbed petite frame, except her hips were slimmer than mine, her eyelashes thick as Joshua's and Nerissa's. When I first went away to college, she was eleven years old, and she saved my fingernail clippings and the glass Coke bottles I drank out of. She was my baby sister. I let myself be weak for a moment. Either she was asleep or she had the grace to pretend that she was asleep, because when I lay behind her and cried, my unsteady breathing the only clue I wept, from dread or relief, she let me. That is how we began our summer.

When we woke, she didn't mention my crying. Instead, we went for a ride in the car. Charine suffered from motion sickness, and air-conditioning made it worse. I wanted to soak in all the heat I could, since my first Michigan winter had stunned me with relentless snow and unyielding cold, so we rode with the windows down in hundred-degree Mississippi heat. We had nothing to do. We rode down to the county park, the swings hanging limp and smelling like singed rubber in the sun, the nets on the basketball hoops still, the bleachers empty. The landscape echoed with loss and grief. We were lonely.

"Let's go chill by Rog," Charine said. "There's always people over there, and he's always home."

*　*　*

Rog lived in a subdvision in Pass Christian called Oak Park. It was mostly Black, and the maze of its streets began at North Street, on the north, and ended on Second Street, in the south, which was around two long blocks away from the beach and the Gulf of Mexico. The houses closer to North Street were standard to most of the subdivisions I've seen in south Mississippi: brick, one story, three bedrooms, a sliver of a concrete slab serving as a porch across the front. The houses that were closer to Second Street, closer to the beach, even by scent and not sight, were larger. Rog and his mother, Phyllis, who everyone called Mrs. P., lived in a house that was closer to North Street.

Rog was short and lean. He was brown as pine bark, and wore braids, and clothes so loose he almost disappeared in them. His eyes were always half lidded, always squinting. His face was narrow and long. His smile was shocking, bright, wide. He smiled a lot.

Rog's father, Roger Eric Daniels II, or Jock for short, had died when he was twenty-eight of a heart attack, so Mrs. P. was the sole caregiver, which meant that Rog, like most of us who grew up without fathers, spent a lot of time with his two older sisters or other kids his age, unsupervised, especially in the summer. One Fourth of July, he and his cousins twisted firecrackers together in a sulfurous bunch, put the firecrackers in mailboxes, and lit them. The mailboxes exploded. Someone called the police. When the police arrived, they told the kids that it was a federal offense to tamper with the mail, and they took the other two boys to a juvenile detention facility. This is how silly pranks by Black kids are handled in the

South, Rog learned. Rog was lucky in some ways: he wasn't caught.

WHEN ROG WAS in seventh grade, he dated my middle sister, Nerissa, for a week. She hadn't become pregnant with my nephew by then, but she soon would. Nerissa'd had curves since she was nine. She had long glossy hair, and one mole on her chin and another on her chest, lined up like buttons; from when she was a toddler, my parents recognized the curse of beauty put on her. *If we ever have to worry about being made grandparents early,* my mother would say of Nerissa, *she's the one.* Nerissa, unlike me, was popular in middle school, had boyfriends. She said she was head over heels for Rog, thought that he was the cutest thing in middle school. They passed notes in class. His asked: *Do you want to go out with me?* My sister replied: *Yes.* She wore big T-shirts she borrowed from Josh, big shorts, and tennis shoes. A year or so later, when she got pregnant for a nineteen-year-old boy from Gulfport, those T-shirts she borrowed from Joshua would hide her growing belly for the first five months.

Nerissa and Rog's romance lasted a week. She was too boyish, with her big shirts and shorts, so Rog broke up with her. But they were still friends. Years later, when she was living in her first apartment, Rog would visit, walk through the front door, throw his arms around her, ask her, "When you going to be my old lady?" Smile.

"You had your chance," Nerissa joked. Rob, her boyfriend, sat on the sofa, with a black cigar in the corner of his mouth, a beer at his side. He smiled, his genial, easy smile, and showed the gold teeth he polished so religiously they shone against his dark face.

"Aw, come on Nerissa, give me another chance," Rog said.

"Nope," Nerissa laughed.

Rog's bedroom was dark: dark walls, dark curtains. He had shelves up, and on his shelves were model cars with shiny chrome wheels on them, so carefully put together, down to the smallest detail. In his stereo, you'd find Tupac. Old No Limit and Fifth Ward Boyz, both out of New Orleans. Cam-ron and Dipset out of New York City. And on his wall, he hung pictures. He was a good artist. In Mississippi, out in the country where there is no concrete or enough buildings crammed closely enough to make a good canvas for graffiti, kids who would normally develop their street art and tag do it like Rog did, by papering their rooms with sketches. Rog drew pictures of cars and some of people. He tried his hand at stylized words. OPT, one piece of artwork said. Another: THUG LIFE. And another: LAUGH NOW, CRY LATER.

Rog dropped out of school in the tenth grade; it's not un-common for young Black men to drop out here. Sometimes they are passively forced out by school authorities, branded as misfits or accused of serious offenses like selling drugs or ha-rassing other students: sometimes they are pushed to the back of classrooms and ignored. Rog sat in the back of one such

class and beat-boxed while his cousins sang spirituals that sub-
stituted the teacher's name for Jesus'. He left school, worked,
and then in 2000 went to Los Angeles to live with his relatives. He loved it. He worked in an auto body shop, made
more money than he would have been able to make in Mississippi, and enjoyed the city: theme parks, roller skating rinks,
the beach, where the water was blue and rushed the palm-
decked shore in waves, so different from our beach, where
the dirty gray Gulf lapped desultorily at a man-made beach
ringed by concrete and pine trees.

Later, I wondered if it was a kindness to Nerissa, a remem-
brance of their short middle school romance, that made Rog
hang out with us during the 2001 Mardi Gras Pass Christian
parade, when he was visiting home. I had been out of college
and without a job for almost a year, but I'd booked a ticket
and flown home from New York City for Mardi Gras. This
added to my considerable credit card debt. I didn't care. I
needed to go home, even if only for three days. My brother
was newly dead. I expected him to be alive every day when
I woke. On that February day, I did not know he was only the
first. It was raining and chilly. We were all subdued, except
Rog. He swaggered between clusters of friends and cousins
from DeLisle and Pass Christian. He stood at the edges of pictures with a haul of big purple and green and gold beads on
his neck, the kind that in normal years we'd plead the loud-
est for the pleasure of wearing them for a day. My sisters and
I huddled under umbrellas and watched the press of people,
ignoring the beads that pelted our umbrellas. My three-year-
old nephew, newly bereft of his uncle and bewildered by the

crowds, hugged my leg. My grief was so great that the sheen of the colorful beads, the music sounding from the floats, the celebration of that day felt like a farce, an insult.

On the day of the first Mardi Gras parade I'd attended after my brother's death, the reality of Joshua's absence was soothed by Rog, his easy smile, his arm casually slung over my or my sisters' shoulders. *Hey,* he said. And then: *What's up?*

I DON'T KNOW why Rog returned home to Mississippi for good in 2002. I imagine that it was because he was home-sick, because he missed the narrow, tree-shaded streets of Pass Christian, the houses scattered here and there and set twelve feet high on stilts to protect them from hurricane storm surges. Maybe he missed Mrs. P., his sisters Rhea and Danielle, his large extended family scattered through Pass Christian and DeLisle, his cousins. Many leave and never come back, lured away by cities where it's easier to find working-class jobs, where opportunity comes easier because those in power are less bound by the culture of the South. But I've heard others who've moved away from Mississippi, worked for five, ten years of their adult lives somewhere else, and then moved back to Mississippi say: "You always come back. You always come back home."

THE FIRST NIGHT Charine and I went to Rog's house in that summer of 2004 after Aldon and I had driven home from Michigan, we didn't go inside. Our cars lined the street, bumper to bumper. The night swooped down in great black swaths, and the streetlights, spaced far apart, shone weakly. Insects swarmed in foggy clouds around the bulbs, dimming them even further so we were dusky shadows, and the stars dozed on the dome of the sky like larger, distant insects.

The boys turned the bass up on their car stereos, and we sat on their trunks and hoods, jiggling to the beat, sweating and sliding down the steel. Rog walked over, his Budweiser in one hand, his other hand waving like a child's slicing through the air out of the passenger window of a car.

"Aaaaawwww," he said, and hugged all three of us at once: me, Tasha, my brother's last girlfriend, and Charine. He half jumped on us. Threw his leg over the row of our feet.

We laughed. We could laugh when we were drunk, even in the summer of 2004.

"All right, Rog," Charine said. "You messing up."

"What you mean?" Rog slid off us.

"I can't feel the trunk with you jumping like that. Do you feel that?" she asked me.

"Like a massage, huh, Charine?" Rog said, and then he passed her a black cigar. "You dead wild."

He danced around the trunk that night, kept us laughing. His smile never disappeared from his narrow face. While the other boys huddled in their cars, having conversations that we were not privy to, discussing and doing things I had no idea they did, Rog held court with us. He reminded me of Aldon. There was something gentle about him, considerate. Good. The first time he saw one of his younger cousins experimenting with weed in the street in front of his house, he stopped him. He walked up to him in the dark and said, "Aw, man, what you doing? You need to cut that out. You don't need to be fucking with it like that." His younger cousin laughed; he was already high.

WE PARTIED INSIDE the house only once that summer. We were drinking. We were always drinking. But it was a different kind of drinking from what we'd done the previous summer. That drinking had been insane, ecstatic. We'd taken shots of Everclear that summer, felt that liquor running through us, thrumming: for this moment, you are young and alive. Live, more. The summer of 2004, we were no longer rebel drinkers, imbibing to break rules, to shit on mores. Now, we were subdued drinkers, drinking to forget. By the summer of 2004, we knew we were old: by the end of the summer, we'd know we had one foot in the grave.

On that night at Rog's house, we'd gotten cases of Budweiser, Rog's favorite beer, and we were playing dominoes, smoking, and talking. Charine, who never drank, decided that she was going to drink instead of smoke that night. I stood in the back room, which felt like a screened-in porch, and talked to my younger cousin Dez, who like most of my younger cousins stood taller than me, so he had to bend over when I spoke. He asked me about my writing, what I was working on, and I told him: a book about twin boys, young men, from a place like DeLisle. He made me feel embarrassed when he praised me in the dark room, under the music, for writing about "real shit," he said. I sipped my beer: I hated the taste of it, but I loved the buzz of it. Charine downed her liquor, drink after drink, until she staggered past me.

"I need to go to the bathroom," she said.

Rog led us down the hallway as I walked Charine through his mother's room to her private bathroom. I turned on the light, and Charine sank to her knees, let her head fall in my lap, and passed out. Unconscious, she threw up. Rog disappeared, then reappeared.

"She all right? She need to drink some water."

"Yeah, she a lightweight," I said, stroking her hair, staring blearily at the yellow rug.

For the two hours we sat on the floor of his mother's bathroom, Charine asleep in my lap, me drinking the last of my warm beer, nursing my dark buzz, Rog came with offerings: one glass of water, two glasses of water, potato chips, bread for Charine's stomach. Charine drank the water but refused the bread and chips, so I ate them. When I'd sobered up enough to drive, Rog helped me bring her out to the car and saw us off into the bayou, the night.

The next day Charine and I visited Rog. The day was hot and bright, cumulus clouds like mountains loomed in the sky, but it did not rain. Rog was sitting in a hard plastic chair, and when Charine and I walked up the driveway to the carport, he dragged over two other chairs, metal with plastic weave. We sat. I was hungover. The woven straps dug into my legs, but it felt good to sit, to find a little ease in the shade as Rog and Charine smoked, as the cicadas trilled and ticked. Rog and Charine talked about how things in the hood had changed, how we felt like death was stalking us, driving us from one another, the community falling apart. They talked about how messed up they'd been the night before. They talked about California. They talked about change.

Rog talked about change, about returning to California,

with others, too. It was all he could think of then, and I imagined the pines and the thick air felt like the walls of an invisible room to him, closed on all sides. Perhaps this made him use more, because like many people, Rog medicated with drugs and alcohol. His habit became more evident. He lost weight, became even more wiry, even more lean, his smile, slight when it shone, dimmer in his face. His cousin Bebe said that leaving was all he talked about one summer day, leaving Mississippi to return to California. He missed his job; he missed the freedom of the different, the new. He told her, "Cuz, you know, it's a better place for me out there. I can make a better way." He turned his bottle up. "I'm ready to change, ready to go," he said. "I'll be straight out there, but here . . ." And as he spoke, a boy from the neighborhood who was notorious for using drugs, cocaine, heroin, marijuana, drove up in his Cutlass. Parked. Walked up and said: "What's up?"

SOME KNEW THAT Rog was snorting cocaine, and others didn't. In Mississippi, cocaine was a party drug in the late seventies and early to mid-eighties. People in my parents' generation snorted it, or they smoked it with weed. They did it secretly, casually. For some the habit stuck, and for others it didn't. And then came crack, a terrible development for those with a coke habit: it was a cheaper, more addictive high. Those who couldn't stop changed from partiers to addicts. They stole from their families, from strangers, to support their habit.

There is a story that I like to tell about the close-knit nature of DeLisle and the Black enclave of Pass Christian. When you wake up and find that, say, your car stereo is missing from your car, you're pissed off about it. You call your cousins and tell them about it, mention it to a few friends. You suspect who may have stolen it. By noon, one of your cousins or friends has called you with news, told you that someone saw someone else walking through the woods or loping along the street with your stuff under their arm. That afternoon, you show up at the thief's house, which is small, a little worn, but neat. You get loud. You demand your radio back. They are shamefaced as you berate them, and they may even curse you back or smile nervously, but they will return what they stole. This is how stealing was handled when I was growing up through the eighties and the beginning of the crack epidemic in the nineties. This is not what happens today. By the time you get to the thief's house in the afternoon, a house that has no electricity and a rotting floor, they will have pawned your radio, and they will have smoked it, and their eyes, jittery in the skull, will slide past you to the red dirt ground, to the sky, to the trees waving overhead, and they will lie until you give up to follow the trail elsewhere, until you leave.

There is a stigma associated with coke among the young in DeLisle and Pass Christian because it is too close a cousin to crack. Kids will take shots of white strong liquor, they will smoke weed wrapped in thick blunts, they will even take Ecstasy or prescription pain pills, but they will not casually pull out an eight-ball of coke and push it across the table at a house party. Why? Because the specter of the cousin or the uncle or aunt or the mother or father who couldn't stop partying, whose teeth are burned brown from the pipe, sits next to them at that table. Young people who do coke lie about it, attempt to hide it, and often fight it. Rog hid it and fought it.

Some of my relatives, on my mother's side and my father's, have abused crack, on and off, for years. *I can't fault them for it,* Charine always says when we talk about it, *that's just their high that they like. Fuck it. It helps them cope.* And then: *They're grown.* I understand her now, but I did not understand her point in the summer of 2004. Did not see the way liquor had been my drug for years. Was not connecting the relief I felt when I drank with the drugs others were using, or even thinking that it could be the same for my relatives, the same for my siblings, or the same for Rog. I knew that I lived in a place where hope and a sense of possibility were as ephemeral as morning fog, but I did not see the despair at the heart of our drug use.

THE LAST TIME that I remember seeing Rog in the summer of 2004 was at a gas station. I don't remember whom I was with, but we'd stopped to get gas at the BP on the beach in Pass Christian, the BP that would disappear a year later when Hurricane Katrina swept in and decimated the coastline. The pumps buzzed, and I jumped out of the car when I saw Rog lope by with his beer, his face long, his mouth closed, no teeth this time. He was so skinny. His eyes were closed to slits like he was smiling, but he was not.

"What up, Rog?" I said.

"What's up?"

He hugged me, black T-shirt loose on his frame. His shoulders barely touched mine. He was already pulling away, already out of the polite embrace. He was already back in the car with two men from the hood. He was already swallowed by the black reach of the highway. The wind from the Gulf stuttered in, blew sand lazily across the parking lot, across my feet, and Rog disappeared into the dim, tree-tunneled streets of Pass Christian, like an animal down its secret hole.

YEARS LATER, CHARINE told me she tried to visit Rog after he died but before he was found. In other words, she visited him when she thought he was alive. She and her friends banged on the door of the dark, shuttered house, not knowing that Rog was already dead inside. His sister Rhea would find him two days later. They called his name: "Rog!" They said, "His ass is probably passed out in there. Rog!" Louder. "Come open the door!"

Now, Charine says, knowing how he lay behind that door breaks something inside of her.

YEARS LATER, NERISSA told me about Rog's visit with her in February 2004. This would have been when Rog and our cousins were doing too much coke because C. J. had just died. This would have been when they were raw with love, with losing. This would have been when Rog passed out, when our cousin was afraid he wasn't breathing, when he carried Rog into Nerissa's bathroom and put him in the tub, ran the water cold, hoping for a miracle, for the flame not to go out. My cousin cried. He yelled, "Don't do this to me!" Beat Rog on the chest. "Not you!" Yelled at Rog, "Not again!" And then Rog drew a breath and opened his eyes.

ROG DID COCAINE, and then he took a few Lortabs on the night of June 3, 2004. For once, there was no party, no casual gathering of friends at his mother's house. Then Rog, the boy with the beautiful smile and the long face, lay back in his bed, feeling high and low, feeling everything and nothing, all at once. Perhaps he was thinking he should be somewhere else, maybe out under the palm trees in California, walking along Venice Beach with his cousins, smelling incense that you could almost mistake for weed. Maybe he thought of the sky over the Pacific Ocean, the water stretching away to meet the clouds and disappear over the horizon, the way it seemed to go on forever. Maybe he was thinking of his family, of his mama's return from working offshore in the Gulf of Mexico on an oil rig. Maybe he was thinking about the air conditioner, how good it was to lie in a cool dark bed at home, to be. Maybe he wasn't thinking about any of these things, but I like to imagine that he was thinking about all of them when the seed of the bad heart that had killed his father sent out roots and bloomed violently in Rog's chest. Sometime that night Rog died of a heart attack.

★ ★ ★

I WAS AT my mother's house, alone, when my brother's last girlfriend, Tasha, called and told me Rog had died.

"They killed my brother!" she sobbed. She'd been close to Rog.

I left my mother's house and drove through DeLisle, deep into the country. I drove with the windows down and my lights low. On a solitary road I ran into my ex-boyfriend from high school, Brandon; we stopped our cars in the middle of the empty darkness that is endemic to rural Mississippi. I'd known Brandon since I was seven years old, and his face was as familiar as my own. I walked to his car and passed a hand over my forehead and leaned into the driver's-side window. His own eyes were wide and black, and the woods around us burned with calling insects.

"You heard?" I said.

I hugged him. Rog was his first cousin, his younger cousin. They had the same black eyes, the same curly black hair. Brandon nodded. My face brushed against his as I pulled away. His skin was wet: the night was so hot I didn't know if it was sweat or tears.

"You heading to Oak Park?" I asked. After days of others knocking but not walking in, Rog's sister Rhea had found Rog. I do not like to imagine what it must have been like for her.

"Yes," Brandon said.

I left him behind in the middle of the street. When I arrived in the Oak Park subdivision, I parked my car on a cement curb and walked over to stand on the lawn in front of Rog's house. People stood in drifting pockets at the edge of the same street we had partied on. Charine and Tasha met me there. We faced the house. A long hearse, gray and black with silver accents, took Rog away. It had a hard time maneuvering the driveway. The street lamps buzzed. When they rolled Rog out on the stretcher and loaded him into the back, I cried, my mouth open. I hated the hearse. I wanted to set it on fire. As the driver clumsily crushed the grass and swerved out of the yard, I thought of what my ex had said to me before I drove away.

"They picking us off, one by one," Brandon had breathed.

After the people dispersed and Rog's immediate family locked the house and turned off all the lights, we milled in the street, waiting. We waited as if we could will the hearse back to the house, will Rog to rise out of the back, alive. Will him to joke, to smile. I drove home across the black, inky bayou by myself. I thought about Josh. I thought about C. J., about Demond, about Ronald. I rode with the windows open and thought about Rog.

I thought about what Tasha and Brandon had said, and I wondered who *they* were. Rog had died by his own hand, by his own heart; were *they* us? Or was there a larger story that I was missing as all these deaths accumulated, as those I loved died? Were *they* even human? My headlights lit a slim sliver in the darkness, and suddenly *they* seemed as immense as the darkness, as deep, as pressing. I turned off my music and rode home without the narrative of song, with only the bugs' shrill cry and hot wind whipping past my window. I tried to hear the narrative in that, to figure out who the *they* that wrote our story might be.

★   ★   ★

AFTER ROG'S FUNERAL, I tapped Rhea's shoulder. I opened my arms, hugged her. Her big, expressive eyes were bloodshot and wandering. I wondered what I would have wanted someone, anyone, to say to me when my brother died, anything beyond *Are you all right?* and *Are you okay?* I knew the answers to those questions. I whispered into her ear: "He will always be your brother, and you will always be his sister."

What I meant to say was this: *You will always love him. He will always love you. Even though he is not here, he was here, and no one can change that. No one can take that away from you. If energy is neither created nor destroyed, and if your brother was here with his, his humor, his kindness, his hopes, doesn't this mean that what he was still exists somewhere, even if it's not here? Doesn't it? Because in order to get out of bed this morning, this is what I had to believe about my brother, Rhea.* But I didn't know how to say that.

AFTER EVERY FUNERAL in the hood, including Rog's, there is a gathering or a repast. Older women brought large pans containing casseroles and meat to Mrs. P.'s house. We all found our way there, and we parked in front of her house, some of us in neighboring yards, our cars half on the grass, half on the asphalt, this time in the middle of the day. We ate with plates balanced on our laps, one foot in our cars, the other out. We smoothed our shirts down, white T-shirts with pictures of Rog framed in blue. In Rog's picture, he has deep dimples and an even, blinding smile. We breathed heavily.

The memorial shirt is most common at funerals for young people. I do not know if it is common in Black neighborhoods in the North or East or West, but in the South, it has become as traditional as the repast. Rog's shirt was made by his cousins: they gathered the pictures for the shirt, designed it, and then offered one to anyone who could afford the $20 it cost to make it. In this way, the young memorialize the young. On his memorial T-shirt, Rog has a charming grin, looks as if he is on the verge of saying, *Hey, how you doing, what we getting into tonight?* Around Rog's larger picture, there are pictures of the other dead young men: Ronald, C. J., Demond, Joshua, and two others who had died years before and whom I was not so close to, one in a car wreck and the other by suicide. They are all smiling in what look like school photos or family reunion shots. My brother looks like a young thug in his picture, like he could run with the best of the phantom menace in New Orleans. He holds my father's SK gun and postures for the camera, a bandana over the bottom half of his face, his hair cut close to his head. He must have been sixteen then. I had never seen this picture of Joshua before, and seeing him there with all the other dead young men made me cry while I ate. I chewed my funeral food on a hot Mississippi summer day and looked at my brother's eyes, large and brown and wide, in a picture that revealed nothing of what he was, and represented everything that he wasn't.

YAGGA YO and WHAT YOU MEAN? it said on the back of Rog's memorial shirt. This was something he said often, I was told, but his cousins did not tell me its meaning. OPT, the shirt also read. Rog's picture was an insult to the living man, too blurry, too static for the smiling, open-armed twenty-three-year-old he'd been. Written on the front of the shirt and finished on the back was the declaration: THE SAME THING THAT MAKE YOU LAUGH MAKE YOU CRY. This was too pat, I thought as I wiped my tears. In that moment, I could not remember ever laughing, could not recall what it felt like to open my mouth and scream my loud, embarrassing laugh with Rog. I looked at my family and friends, all of us crying and looking away from each other, and I could not recall having the ability to laugh at all. Only this loss, this pain. I could not understand why there was always this.

WE ARE BORN
1977–1984

I was born early at six months, on April Fools' Day, 1977. My mother was eighteen, my father twenty. They were living with my father's mother in Oakland, in his childhood room awash with the detritus of his teen years: Bruce Lee posters, nunchaku hung on nails, my father's illustrations. My mother cannot remember the conversation that signaled my impending arrival, but I imagine my mother waking and telling my father, "I need to go to the hospital," and my father laughing, thinking it a good April Fools' joke. And then my mother would have curled over in pain on the bed. "I'm serious." The look on her face: his doe catching a glancing blow from a car fender.

When I was born, I weighed two pounds and four ounces, and the doctors told my parents I would die. My skin was red, paper thin, and wrinkly, my eyes large and alien. My father took a picture of me, of my entire body, cupped in the palm of his hand. Because I weighed so little, I developed blood tumors, which swelled up and out: they were bulbous, swollen maroon, an abundance of blood barely contained by thin skin. Two burst and leaked. When I was around four years old, they would shrink completely flat and leave mottled scars where they'd sprouted and grown: on my stomach, my wrist, the back of my thigh. I had a growth in my abdomen, so the doctors sliced me open millimeters below my belly button for exploratory surgery before sewing me closed. The incision must have been done across the whole length of my small belly, and I imagine myself open like a frog on the operating table. Over the years, the scar would stretch, dimple, and pull where the stitches had been sewn. When the doctors realized I would survive, they told my parents I would have severe developmental problems. They were surprised that my lungs worked well, that I fought to breathe. *She has a strong heart*, they said. In another picture, the skin under my eyes wells in red bags, and my mother holds a breathing tube to my face. I look weary. I lived, silent and tenacious, in my incubator, my body riddled with multiple tubes. During the two months I lived at the hospital, my red color leached away. I slowly gained weight on my stomach, my gamy legs, my outstretched arms. My eyes shrank into my head. The medical staff discharged me, yellow, bald, fat, and scarred, on May 26, 1977: my mother's nineteenth birthday.

We moved out of my grandmother's house into our own one-bedroom apartment. I sprouted hair on my head, which grew half an inch, black and fine and curly, and stopped. It would not grow again until I turned three. In pictures of me from that time, my mother combed my hair forward in a silken cap in an effort to frame my face, to make me look more like a girl. In a picture from my second birthday, I am dressed in a long-sleeved red cotton peasant-style shirt, thick with maroon embroidery, and black pants. Red was the color my mother chose to dress me in, again and again: no pink or blue or green or purple, but red. Red as the blood tumors. I was not a pink girl. In one photograph, we are high in the hills above Berkeley and Oakland, dirt and yellow grass behind me. The dust in the dry hills makes the air look golden. I look healthy, like a beautiful boy. Most of the tumors, which were just beginning to shrink from their skin stretching red, were hidden by my outfit. My expression is serious as I gaze at the person behind the camera.

MY FATHER ALWAYS told me he felt insulted when the doctors informed them that I would die. The doctor ignored me in the incubator, my head turned to the side, my lungs aflutter through the thin skin of my chest, and faced my parents and said: "Chances are she won't survive."

Daddy didn't say anything. He stood there holding my mother's hand. She would not cry until she could do so alone. There were a lot of things the doctors said to my mother and father when I was born, about my birth, the likelihood of my death, that they did not understand. Things they would not remember later when I asked them for the story. They were young and poor and Black in Oakland in the late seventies. My father waited until the doctor left, fit his solid hand into the plastic glove sealed into the side of the incubator, and brushed my tiny hand with one finger. He could not put his pointer finger in my palm for me to grab, since his finger was the size of my arm.

"I wanted to tell them you were a fighter," he told me when I was a teenager. "I wanted to tell them that my baby wasn't going to die because she was a warrior."

We come from a line of men and women who have fought hard to live. My maternal grandmother, Dorothy, raised seven children on her own in a two-bedroom, one-bathroom house. Over the years, she worked and saved and transformed those two bedrooms into four. She held jobs as a maid, a hairdresser, a seamstress, and finally a factory worker at a pharmaceutical plant. "We need a woman who can work like a man." My grandmother got that factory job after a man saw her lift and carry a full-grown hog on her shoulders. The men in my family have worked for decades as gardeners, carpenters, factory men, bootleggers, and shop owners, and have built houses from the ground up with their own hands.

My father said he knew even then that I would not disappoint.

I CAN REMEMBER little of those first three years in the Bay Area. My father had been a hellion before my mother and I showed up. He was picked up in raids when the police would target all the members of his gang for suspected drug activity, for scuffles with other gangs over narrow sidewalks, small roads. There were tens of them in holding cells, yelling at the police, shaking their heads, laughing, talking shit to each other: *What did you do? Naw, man, what did you do?* The artist in him fell in love with Jimi Hendrix; he put chemicals in his hair so that he could wear an afro, an afro that fell instead of stood. He was offered a scholarship at an art school when he finished high school, but he chose not to attend; he had his mother and his seven siblings to think of, so he worked. He worked at gas stations in ailing neighborhoods where prostitutes walked up and down the street. He treated them well, let them use the bathroom without buying anything from the store, joked with them while they were waiting for customers. On weekends, he went to drag races in Fresno with his friends and tripped on acid. But when my mother came to California, he slowed down some. He stayed home more, but his new domestic life with my mother didn't prevent him from straying. Remaining faithful to my mother required a kind of moral discipline he'd never developed, since it was constantly undermined by his natural gifts: his charm, his sense of humor, his uncommon beauty. My mother fought with him about it, but this only made him cleverer and sneakier about his cheating, even as he said all the things my mother wanted to hear. *Neither of us had daddies, so of course we going to be a family. Of course I'm going to be here.* My mother was taking community college classes and working at my preschool during those years. She wanted to major in early education, to be a preschool teacher.

My father said that she was shaped like a Coke bottle, and that she was beautiful. I have seen pictures of her from those days, and she *was* beautiful: sharp cheekbones and nose, large eyes, long silky hair that ran over her shoulders and down her back like water, and a tiny mole at the corner of her mouth. When she brought me to the grocery store, people complimented her on her beauty, on me, her adorable baby boy. *She's a girl,* my mother said. Eventually, she heard me called a boy so much that she stopped correcting admiring strangers.

I was walking by then. I was two. I had a fat belly, short legs, large dark eyes. The silken cap of hair. My father and mother had a party, the kind of party one has for no other reason than to share a good time with loved ones. My mother put me in a green jumper, and I toddled around my father's legs, his cousins' legs, my mother's, my fathers' sisters'. They picked me up, a miracle baby, and kissed me on my cheeks, which were still fat as ripe peaches. I walked to my room, pulled on a pair of cowboy boots and a cowboy hat my mother bought for me.

"What you doing, Mimi?" That was my nickname. The upstairs neighbor in our apartment complex called her daughter that, and my mother liked the name so much she stole it for me. I jumped on my steel rocking horse, set up in the corner, careful to not pinch my legs in the springs, and I began rocking back and forth, squeaking against the chatter of the drinking and smoking adults. They laughed. As the party wore on, I picked up cans when the adults weren't looking, sometimes when they were, and sipped the dregs of their beer before they took the cans from me with a *No, Mimi*. My mother took a picture of me while I held a can to my belly, beer dribbling from my chin, the can half the length of my torso, before taking it away. In the picture, I'm grinning, my feet planted wide, almost proud. I was part of the party.

MY FATHER REMEMBERS those days better than my mother, or he is more open about them, or he is more nostalgic for them, which is why he talks about them with me and my mother doesn't. Despite his pleasant memories, when we lived in California he missed home, he said. My mother didn't. She wanted to stay in California. She's told me less about that time, but she says she liked the freedom of it, the vista of the cities rolling themselves out over the hills. There were no vistas in Mississippi, only dense thickets of trees all around. You could only see the closest house, the dog chained to a tree, your brother riding his bike by on the dirt road. At night, perhaps, a snatch of stars: in the day time, the leaden rain-heavy clouds closed in. But in California, my mother could look out over the horizon and watch the sun rise in the east, and then she could watch it set out over the mammoth Pacific in the west. In California, my family sat at the center of those hills, and my mother could tend to her husband and her child only, free of family and the South.

When I attended college in the Bay Area, I missed the Mississippi air. I wonder if my father felt the same, if the steady cold of the bay made him miss the close heat of Mississippi. When my father brought up the idea of moving back home, my mother balked. They argued over it. But eventually my mother relented because she loved my father. She was also pregnant with my brother by then, and perhaps she wanted the support of her family if she was to have a second child. It was 1980. I was three.

My father and mother packed all of their possessions into their cars, a station wagon and a lowrider Riviera, and we made the long drive down California to L.A. on I-5, then crossed the desert Southwest on I-10. Somewhere in Arizona, my mother, big with my brother, walked into a grocery store and fainted. Our cars had no air-conditioning, yet she still drove those twenty-three hundred miles, her mouth set, my brother large and kicking in her stomach, his feet separated from the metal link of the Riviera's chain steering wheel by the thin balloon of her fat and skin, windows down, wind blowing. I lay curled in the passenger seat in that car. As my mother drove through the burning desert, I slept, dreaming burning dreams. We sped through the long, seemingly endless stretch of Texas to the blooming green of Louisiana, and finally to DeLisle: home.

ONE DAY MY brother wasn't there, and the next day he was. He was born at Memorial Hospital in Gulfport, Mississippi. He was yellow and fat, his eyes large and liquid. His mouth gaped with gums. Sometimes my mother let me sit in a chair and hold him, his body stretching from my shoulder down and across my legs. I remember snippets of him as a baby, but not enough to grow him from infant to toddler in the narrative of his life. Joshua was born on time at nine months, but he wasn't an easy delivery. My mother says he was born looking at a sky he could not yet see: sunny-side up, the doctor called it. The doctor turned Joshua facedown in my mother's womb, three times. Every time, my mother said, she felt him turning to face the world again, as if he knew from the first that he wanted to see for himself. He was a beautiful baby: sandy skin, dark brown hair that later fell out and grew in blond. One day he isn't there, and the next day he is. And just like that, I'm his big sister.

Once home, we moved often. We lived in a small white two-bedroom house in Pass Christian, but our life there is fuzzy in my memory. We then moved to a small blue house, this one a three-bedroom, built on my great-grandmother Ellen's land in DeLisle where my father had played as a child and lost his eye. The house was built on cinder blocks, so the steps seemed impossibly high to me, and it was in a corner of the field. The field seemed immense. Mother Ellen's house, small and faded gray, sat three hundred yards away, and the woods bordering the field clung closely to the back and sides of the house. There was a small chicken coop under the trees behind our house, and my father put two doghouses out on the other side for our dogs: one a black pit bull called Homeboy, and the other a short white pit bull mix called Mr. Cool.

I grew taller. My mother combed my hair up into multiple pigtails, secured them with large plastic bobs we called knockers. When I slept at night, they dug into my scalp. By the time I was five, my brother was three, and he came up to my waist. He wanted us to be a team, but when my mother had somewhere to go and my father stayed home and watched us, I left my brother and walked up the long drive that led to the road and played with my cousin Farrah. We played house and snuck to watch TV under the curtain that her father tacked in the doorway between the kitchen and the living room. Sometimes we played in the field that separated our houses, and one such day my brother came looking for me. He could walk easily now, and his blond afro bloomed. He wore a diaper and nothing else. He walked from one end of the railless front porch to the other, looking off into the grass. He stopped at the edge of the steps, turned around, angled one leg behind him until he found the top step, and then slid the rest of the way down so he stood on that step before turning in a circle to face the yard again.

"Mimi!" Joshua called.

I ducked lower so that only my eyes showed over the brick. I watched him. I did not want to call back, to have him come

out into the yard, to have to take care of him instead of playing my game.

"Mimi!" Josh yelled.

He was so skinny, only his belly round as a ball. I did not
say anything. He looked out in wonder over the yard, which
must have seemed even larger to him than it did to me: it was
a vast stretch of overgrown grass, and then those silent houses
in the murky distance where his sister had disappeared.

My father slammed out of the front door. He was in shorts
and nothing else. He had probably been asleep. He grabbed
my brother by one arm, yanked him so he dangled in the air,
and began whipping him.

"Boy! What I told you about going outside by yourself!"

My brother wailed, turning in circles like a sinker on a
fishing line. My father's hand whacked my brother's diaper
again and again, and I was afraid. I'd seldom seen my father
angry, violent. I could not understand why Daddy was so upset with Joshua, could not understand what lesson my father
was trying to teach my brother. I could not understand why
Joshua dangled like a baby doll. And even today, that whipping he received feels like my fault. I'm still ashamed that I
did not step out of that dense grass, that I did not climb those
steps and grab his hand and lead him down them as an elder
sister should, that I did not say: *Here I am, brother. I'm here.*

MY FATHER WAS not usually quick-tempered. He dealt with
me mostly with forbearance and tenderness; he never whipped
me. But he whipped my brother. He was stricter with him.
With Joshua, my father's patience was thin. There was no

room for error in disciplining my brother, my father thought, because my brother was a boy. A son. A child who would be harder pressed to be a fighter, even more than the girl who'd been born early with the strong heart. My brother would have to be stronger than that. My brother would have to grow up and be a Black man in the South. My brother would have to fight in ways that I would not. Perhaps my father dreamed about the men in his family who died young in all the wrong ways, and this forced his hand when he woke to my brother standing next to my parents' bed: pink-mouthed and grinning, green to the world, innocent.

When he wasn't disciplining Joshua, my father was playful. When my mother left us home with him one evening, after he'd had a long day of work, my father covered himself with a blanket and crouched in the middle of the mattress. Joshua and I clutched each other. We skittered around the corners of the room as my father scuttled from side to side under the blanket. He circled the bed, following us, making strange guttural noises. Joshua and I laughed. We were breathless. We tiptoed closer to the bed, and my father swiped an arm out, a great knuckle-scarred claw, and we shrieked, the joy and terror rising in our throats, almost choking us. We darted away. My father played with us until we grew frazzled in the hot room. The sweat ran down our small bodies, our hair alive on our heads, standing in dense halos. At the end of the night, my father snatched us both under the covers with him and tickled us. We yelled for mercy.

On weekday mornings before my father went to work at the glass factory in Gulfport, the family would have breakfast together. My father would turn up the radio in the kitchen.

It was 1982 and my mother was pregnant with my sister Nerissa. New Edition crooned; Joshua and I loved New Edition. My father would grab my hand, and then he'd grab Joshua's, and I'd grab Joshua's small moist palm in my own, and we'd dance in a ring in the middle of the kitchen. My mother shook her head at us, smiled, waved my father away when he tried to get her to dance with him. She would have been feeling pressure then as her family grew, as my father continued to cheat and plead his innocence and devotion and cheat more. She was afraid of what she saw on the horizon. She could not dance in the kitchen. She fried our eggs sunny side up, and as a family, we sat at the table and ate.

BUT MY FATHER could be dark, too. He was attracted to violence, to the basic beauty of fighting, the way it turned his body and those he fought into meticulously constructed machines. He taught his purebred pit bull to fight with deflated bike tires. Alternately he coddled his dog, treated it as tenderly as one of his children, but the dog's ability to fight was paramount, and my father had little mercy for him in his quest to make him harder to kill. Like my brother, my father's dog required a hard hand if he would be his toughest.

My father stood in the doorway of the house with a machete in his hand, the blade so dark gray it looked black. He held it lightly, loosely. My mother was in her room watching television, and Joshua and I crowded around my father's legs, looking out at the yard, at Homeboy, squat and as finely muscled as my father. Homeboy gleamed black and panted with his tongue out. He smiled at us.

"Stay inside," my father said, and he trotted down the steps. Joshua and I dug into the door jamb, waited until Daddy walked around the house, leading Homeboy by his studded collar, to lean far out. We were determined to watch. One of my father's first cousins, also shirtless in white shorts, grabbed Homeboy's tail, held it down still and tight over a pillar of cinder blocks. Homeboy waited patiently, quietly, glanced back over his shoulder, and then snapped at a gnat. He trusted my father. Daddy whipped the machete up and brought it down hard on Homeboy's tail, inches below where the tail merged into his backside. Blood spurted across the gray cinder in a steady gush. Homeboy yelped and jerked. My father dropped the machete and tied a bandage around Homeboy's stump, and then smoothed his sides. Homeboy whimpered and quieted.

"Good boy," my father said. Homeboy licked my father's hand, butted him with his head.

Later, Joshua and I lay in our room, a room that was still decorated only for me; there were Cinderella curtains at the windows, and a rough Cinderella bedspread on my twin bed. When we moved in, Joshua had had his own room, but when my father decided he wanted a room for his weight bench and his kung-fu weapons, they moved Joshua into my room. This made me angry for a week or so because I felt territorial; this was my space. But that night Joshua and I lay quietly in our small beds, Joshua breathing softly, almost snoring, while I lay awake and listened to my father and his cousin in the other room, listened to them take smoking pipes down off the wall where my father had mounted them for decoration, listened to the clink of the weights, all this drifting down the hot hallway in the dark. The wind blew my curtains; they wafted out and stilled. The humid air coming into all the open windows of the house drew the smell of weed into my room. I knew this was some sort of smoke, like cigarettes. My father smoked it and my mother didn't. Maybe my father and his cousin talked about their dogs. Maybe they talked about their cars. Maybe they whispered about women.

MY MOTHER HAD given birth to Nerissa by then. She'd also come to realize the hopelessness of her dreams that our growing family would bind my father to her and encourage his loyalty to her. She'd carried Nerissa to term, and my sister had been a hard birth. She'd been the heaviest of all of us, and had refused to descend down the birth canal, so the doctors and nurses had to drive her out of my mother by taking their forearms and sweeping down my mother's stomach from rib cage to hip, and then grabbing Nerissa's head with forceps. *She didn't want to leave me,* my mother says. When Nerissa was born, she looked the most like my father: she had black hair and large, black eyes shaped like quotation marks in her face when she smiled.

The violence of my sister's birth and the slow unraveling of our family marked my mother when she came home. She was more withdrawn. She turned inward. When her patience waned, she argued with my father over his infidelities, and while my father was dramatic and flamboyant with his anger, flipping mattresses from beds, my mother was curt. I imagine she wanted to spare us the spectacle of their arguments, the way violence hovered at the edges of their confrontations. They never touched each other in anger, but the small things in that house suffered.

THAT YEAR, THE world outside our house taught me and my brother different lessons about violence. Our play taught us that violence could be sudden, unpredictable, and severe, soon.

My mother's brother took Joshua for a ride on his moped. Uncle Thomas was around nineteen, and his moped was white with a maroon seat. My brother sat on my uncle's lap, and my uncle whooped and hollered as they rode in circles around the yard. My uncle had the kind of face that was so hard when he was serious that I could hardly believe it was the same face when he smiled. I wanted a turn on the moped. Joshua leaned forward and grabbed the handlebars, and pretended to steer. The moped accelerated. My uncle clicked the clutch so he could slow down while my brother pressed the gas, and they surged forward. My uncle cut the wheel to stop and they crashed in the sandy ditch. Joshua screamed. Blood ran steadily from his mouth. My uncle apologized again and again: *I'm sorry I'm sorry I'm sorry,* he said. My mother held Josh's mouth wide to look inside and saw that the thin film of flesh that held his tongue to the floor of his mouth had been ripped. They made him suck on ice to dull the pain, to bring the swelling down. His sobs subsided and he went to sleep. They did not take him to the hospital. Perhaps they thought it would heal on its own, or they were afraid of the bill, or they were distracted by their failing relationship. Regardless, the slice healed.

My own lesson in sudden violence involved pit bulls, of course. My father had just purchased a full-grown white pit bull from another man in DeLisle; the dog's name was Chief. One of my father's dogs, Mr. Cool, the gentle white half-breed pit bull who'd comforted me when I was younger, had recently gotten sick. My cousin Larry had taken him out into the backyard into the deep woods behind the house with a rifle in hand, a job my father didn't have the heart to do himself. My father planned to fight the new dog, Chief, along with Homeboy, whom he'd had since he was a puppy. This new dog was twice Mr. Cool's size and less interested in my father's human brood. Homeboy could be tender like Mr. Cool. He would shield me with his body, while Chief looked at me, unmoved.

On an unexceptional hot and bright day, I met Farrah and her brother Marty in the middle of the gravel driveway. Homeboy was asleep under the house. A stray girl dog trotted around us. Chief wandered over to investigate her. He stood to her side very stiffly, smelled her rear, her tail, her belly. He found something to interest him. Both of them stood still before me, entranced with each other. The sun was high. I was hot and cross, and Chief stood in my way.

"Move," I said.

Chief's ear twitched.

"Move, Chief!"

Farrah laughed.

"Move!" I said, and I hit Chief on his broad white back.

He growled and leapt at me. I fell, screaming. He bit me,

again and again, on my back, in the back of my head, on my ear; his stomach, white and furry, sinuous and strong, rolled from side to side over me. His growl drowned all sound. I kicked. I punched him with my fists, left and right, over and over again.

Suddenly he was off me, yelping, running away with his back curved. My great-aunt Pernella, who lived in the smallest house in the field, was beating Chief away with a yellow broom. She picked me up off the ground. I wailed.

"Go home," she told Marty and Farrah.

She placed a palm tenderly where my neck met my back, and she walked me down the long drive to our house. My head and back and arms were burning, red, hotter than the day. Walking was a scream. My mother stood in the doorway of our house. I was barefoot: blood plain on my face and streaming down my body to my feet. The back of my shirt was torn and turning black. Years later, my mother told me, "I saw him attacking you in front of Pernella's house, saw her beating him off. I couldn't move." She was paralyzed by fear.

"The dog. It bit Jesmyn," my aunt said.

Her voice freed my mother from her shock. She called my father, who turned on the water in the bathtub. He picked me up, put me in the water. I hollered. The water turned red. My mother pulled off my shirt, took the cup she kept near the tub to rinse us with when she gave us a bath and poured water over my head. The cuts and gashes sizzled. I screamed.

"We have to wash you off, Mimi," they said. "It's okay."

My mother bloodied her towels as they dried me off, and when she dressed me, I bled through my T-shirt. My father drove us to the hospital. Joshua sat quietly and solemnly in the passenger seat. My mother and I sat in the back of the car, and I lay my head on her lap; my mother laid her hands lightly on the cotton towel they'd wrapped around my head, the cotton staining red. At the hospital, a nurse, tall and White, said to me: "Oh, you got bit by a dog, did you?" My wounds throbbed, and I thought she was stupid. What did she think had happened? When the doctors gave me a rabies shot, they called in four men, and each held one of my five-year-old limbs. I bucked against them. Afterward, they sewed me up. I had three deep puncture wounds on my back. I had a three-inch gash running from the top of my left ear, parallel to my collarbone, back to the nape of my skull. They did not sew any of these. These they disinfected and bandaged. What they did sew was the bottom of my left ear, which had been ripped nearly off, and which hung on by a centimeter of flesh and skin.

"A pit bull did this?" the doctor asked.

"Yes," my father said.

"She fought," my mother said.

"These dogs go for the neck," the doctor said. "If she hadn't fought . . ."

"I know," my father said.

My parents brought me home and I crept around the house. Cousins and neighbors visited. Marty brought my mother the small gold hoop earring I'd worn in my left ear, which he'd found in the bloody gravel. When my father stood in the middle of a gathering of boys and men in the front yard, some who leaned on the hoods of their cars, some who squatted on the ground, some who stood like my father, some of whom were young as fourteen, some of whom were old as sixty, my father said that if I had not fought, I would have died. He said the dog had been trying to rip out my throat. He said the girl dog must have been in heat, and Chief must have thought I was a threat. All of the men held rifles, some like babies in the crooks of their elbows, some thrown over their shoulders. My father dispersed the men, and they went off to hunt the dog: he'd been slinking around the neighborhood, trying to find his way back home. My father found him and shot Chief in the head and buried him in a ditch. I did not tell them that I had started the fight. That I had smacked Chief on his back. I felt guilty. Now, the long scar in my head feels like a thin plastic cocktail straw, and like all war wounds, it itches.

MY DOG BITES had healed to pink scars when my mother and father had their last fight in that house, and it must have been spring because the windows were open. We were preparing to move again, this time to the small trailer that we would live in for a year, my parents by degrees driving each other to even more misery, my brother and sister and I the happiest we'd ever been in our young lives, ignorant of their fights because my parents became so adept at hiding their arguments from Nerissa and Joshua and me. But that night in 1984, they broke and could not contain their ire, my father because he felt shackled by the fact that he had a wife and kids who needed loyalty and fortitude, and my mother because my father had told her he could give us those things, and she was realizing he couldn't. By that time, he'd had his first child out of wedlock. With that, my mother was realizing that soon her mother's story would be hers.

My parents were screaming at each other, their voices loud and carrying out of the windows, but I could not understand what they were saying. I heard one word repeated over and over again: *you. You* and *you* and *you* and *you!* This was punctuated by throwing things. The sun had set, and the evening sky was fading blue to black. Above Joshua's and my head, bats swooped, diving for insects. The windows shone yellow. Nerissa, one year old then, was in the house with our parents, and she was crying. Joshua and I sat on the dark porch, and I held him around his thin shoulders. He was shaking, and I was shaking, but we could not cry. I hugged my brother in the dark. I was his big sister. My mother and father yelled at each other in the house, and as the bats fluttered overhead, dry as paper, I heard the sound of glass shattering, of wood splintering, of things breaking.

DEMOND COOK

BORN: MAY 15, 1972
DIED: FEBRUARY 26, 2004

I NEVER KNEW Demond when he was younger. I came to know him as an adult, when he was old enough to have sharp smile lines and the thin skin at his temples was threaded through with veins. The skull beneath looked hard.

I met Demond when Nerissa lived in a large two-bedroom apartment in Long Beach. Nerissa was the first of the four of us to leave home and rent her own place in Mississippi. I was the eldest and the first to move away a distance, but in some ways Nerissa had been the first to grow up, the first to cut ties with our mother and leave her house. She had little choice. My mother had kicked her out after they'd repeatedly disagreed on Nerissa's mothering of De'Sean, who by then was three years old. De'Sean was a brown boy with a flat nose he inherited from his nineteen-year-old father and a ready smile filled with teeth like candy, small and perfect. Nerissa was the middle girl, taking on the middle child role, and once when we were all younger, Joshua had told her in an argument: "Mama and Daddy love you the least. All of us are special: Mimi's the oldest, Charine's the youngest, and I'm the only boy—think about it." And even though this wasn't true, it colored Nerissa's sense of self and made her want to act out, to be special to someone: her parents, the boys drawn to her by her beauty and her funny, casual coolness. We have a tight bond, we three sisters, which meant that both Charine and I spent days at Nerissa's first apartment, sleeping on old couches our cousin Rhett had given her. I was sitting at the glass table my mother'd given Nerissa as a housewarming gift, after they'd reconciled, when Demond walked in the front door with Rob, Nerissa's longtime boyfriend.

Demond was around five foot ten, and he had my brother's coloring: tan, light brown hair, but he was shorter-limbed and more compact in the chest. He was mostly muscle, where my brother had been softer, still losing his preteen baby fat. Demond wore his hair in dreads that swung and brushed his shoulders when he spoke.

"What's up, Pooh?" This was Rob's nickname for Nerissa while they were dating. Demond put a cigarette in the corner of his mouth, lit it, talked around it.

"What's up, Demond?" Nerissa said. Demond smiled at her and put his arm around her. He was yet another of Rob's friends that she was close to: they confided in her because they liked her dimples, her smile, her warmth and openness. They told her their secrets, and she kept them. She embodied femininity in the way she sat, legs crossed, toes painted and polished, a bundle of curves, and then sullied it with the way she cussed easily and made them laugh.

I was drinking a beer. There were many beers in the apartment that year: cold bottles in tight brown sleeves on counters, on tables, leaning in loose hands on laps, on sofa arms. It was 2003. We'd gone crazy. We'd lost three friends by then, and we were so green we couldn't reconcile our youth with the fact that we were dying, so we drank and smoked and did other things, because these things allowed us the illusion that our youth might save us, that there was someone somewhere who would have mercy on us. We drank Everclear in shots in cars loud with beat under overcast, dark-smothered skies, night after night. My cousins turned the hot tip of blunts to the insides of their mouths, exhaled, pushing smoke out into each other's mouths. *This is what it means to live,* we thought.

"This is my sister Mimi," Nerissa said. She nodded at me, and I smiled over my bottle.

"Hey."

I'd let the beer turn flat, warm, but I'd still drink it. *I am happy,* I thought. And then: *This is what it means to be spared.*

DEMOND HAD GROWN up in DeLisle. Not only was he unusual because he was an only child, but he was also unusual among my generation because he had both parents, and both of his parents had solid working-class jobs. His mother spent years at the pharmaceutical bottling company where he would later work. Being an only child and having a two-parent family meant Demond was the kid in the neighborhood who had all the things the other kids wanted: a swimming pool, an adjustable basketball hoop. Even when we were children, Demond's house was the house where all the kids wanted to be. While my brother and sisters and I were too young and lived too far away to enjoy his family's largesse, the older boys in the neighborhood spent hours at Demond's, swimming away afternoons, wrestling in the water until they smelled strongly of chlorine, their eyes and skin burning. Or sweating for hours in the Mississippi heat, hurling the ball toward Demond's basketball hoop. When Demond graduated from high school, he joined the military. He enlisted in the army for four years, but at some point in his stint he decided that the military was not for him, so he returned home to DeLisle.

Demond was a hustler in the traditional definition of the word, in the way that many, younger and older in DeLisle, were made to be by necessity. He would do what he had to do to support himself and, later, his family. He learned trades as he went. Whatever the project called for, he did: once he worked as a carpenter even though he had few of those skills. For a longer amount of time he worked at a clothing factory; everyone from DeLisle called it the "T-shirt factory." They didn't only manufacture T-shirts there but also acid-washed jeans that were too big in the crotch and too tight in the legs. It was hot in the building, made hotter by fans circulating the dense air. His last job would be in the pharmaceutical factory his mother worked in. The factory was cavernous: long assembly lines snaked through the space, carrying bottles of Pepto-Bismol and capsules of Alka-Seltzer past the workers, who covered their hair with plastic caps and wore thick plastic glasses and face masks. Their jobs were tedious and repetitive, and consisted of bottling the product, screwing caps on, loading the bottles in boxes and onto pallets. This was one of the last good factory jobs on the coast, since the glass bottling company next door had closed years before. The economy of the Gulf Coast had changed drastically in the late eighties and early nineties; many factories had closed, and the seafood industry offered fewer opportunities for employment. As the economy ailed, the Mississippi legislature passed gaming laws that introduced casinos on barges. In general, there was a move from manufacturing and making things to service and tourism. And Black people in the region, who historically did not have the resources to attend college and so did not qualify for the administrative positions, were limited to jobs as cocktail waitresses, valet attendants, and food preparers. Demond was lucky to have his job. At the pharmaceutical plant in Gulfport, he worked different shifts: sometimes overnight, sometimes during the morning and into the afternoon, and sometimes during the afternoon and into the early evening. Most of the time when I saw him he was in throwaway tees, work pants, boots, with a bandana tied around his dreads to hold them away from his face, to protect them from whatever machines he worked over in that factory. He wore his work jumpsuits and his boots like a badge of honor, and when I saw him in them, dusted with whatever compound he packaged in that factory, he looked so much like my brother when he'd flitted from factory job to factory job that it was hard to keep my gaze on him.

DEMOND LIVED IN a seafoam-green house. It had belonged to his grandmother; her husband had probably built it for her, as was the custom in DeLisle in those days. When his girlfriend gave birth to their child when he was in his late twenties, his mother gave him the house for them to live in. It was like most of the older houses in DeLisle: perched up on cinder

blocks, two or three, in case of flood; low ceilings, wood pan-
eling, small corner kitchen. Demond's house was set at the
rear of a long, roomy piece of corner property. His yard was
mostly grass with a few trees clustered closer near the front of
the house: an old spreading oak, pecan, a crape myrtle gone
to seed. The house was fronted by a wood-framed, screened-
in porch. The living room was always dark, lit only by the
neon play of the television across the walls, our faces. The
dining room was usually empty except for domino and spades
games on the older wooden table, the kitchen brown as the
rest of the house. The bathroom was shoved behind the kitchen
in a weird, diagonally placed nook off his child's bedroom.
The rest of the house, which included two more bedrooms,
was designed like a shotgun house, each room opening onto
another.

I never went through the door in his child's bedroom wall
into the bedroom he shared with his girlfriend, through that
door to the extra bedroom in the back where sometimes his
girlfriend's twin slept. I wondered about those rooms often,
wondered if they were as dark as the rooms in the front, if
they seemed as sealed, as insular, and I imagined them stretching off into a great distance, room after room, each one more
cavelike than its predecessor, each holding what would later
become treasure: a picture of Demond grinning and holding
his child, his Enyce fits, his Timberland boots, still smelling
faintly of the sweat of his feet. I never imagined people in
those rooms since all the living seemed to be done in the
front.

We were young people living in houses seemingly more
populated by ghosts than by the living, with the old dead and

the new. I wondered about Demond's grandmother and her kids, and wondered what their lives in Demond's house had been like. Had they lived with the dead as we did? Had they quaffed shine the way we did beer and weed and pills, and then stare at each other in the dim light, glassy-eyed, hoping for a sea change? Even though Demond's parents had remained married and both had good jobs, his family wasn't so different from my family, his reality the same, death stalking us all. If Demond's family history wasn't so different from my own, did that mean we were living the same story over and over again, down through the generations? That the young and Black had always been dying, until all that was left were children and the few old, as in war?

THAT SAME SUMMER, we decided to have a crawfish boil at Nerissa's apartment. Rob borrowed a gas burner and a huge silver pot from a friend in the neighborhood. He set it at the edge of Nerissa's small concrete back patio, pulled out a plastic table, set six chairs around it. It was a bright, warm day; the grass was tough with water because it was summer. It had been raining at least every other day for the past month. Rob set out with two empty coolers and went to a seafood shop that specialized in crawfish during the season, and returned with them full and crawling with mud-green crawfish. He and Nerissa chopped seasonings, dumped them in the heavy silver pot so large an infant could fit inside, and began boiling the sides. Charine and her boyfriend, C. J., cuddled on the sofa, demanded that the rest of us watch the Bruce Lee biopic *Dragon* over and over again. People arrived one by

one, in pairs, in carfuls, Rog and Demond among them.
Once there, Demond took a seat at the table where a dominoes game was in mid-slap. A cooler of beer appeared, a few
bottles of Crown, some fruity malt beverages for the girls.
We spread newspaper over the kitchen table inside the house,
dumped the boiled crawfish, now blood red, on the table. We
peeled, sucked, and ate. My lips began to burn and I noticed
that everyone who was eating crawfish was sniffing, eyes watery, lips red and puffy as pickled pig's lips in a jar. Demond
sat at the table with Nerissa and me and Charine, passed us
drinks, asked me questions about what I did.

"So what you doing up there?"

"I'm trying to be a writer."

"What you want to write?"

"Books about home. About the hood."

"She writing about real shit," Charine said.

"What you mean?" Demond asked.

"They be selling drugs in the book," Charine said.

"For real?" Demond asked, took a swig of his beer.

"Yeah," I said. Laughed, drank a third of my bottle.

"I told you she be writing about the hood," Charine said.

"You should write about my life," Demond said.

"I should, huh?" I laughed again. I heard this often at
home. Most of the men in my life thought their stories,
whether they were drug dealers or straight-laced, were worthy of being written about. Then, I laughed it off. Now, as I
write these stories, I see the truth in their claims.

"It'd be a bestseller," Demond said.

"I don't write real-life stuff," I said. It was my stock response for that suggestion, but even as I said it, I experienced

a sort of dissonance. I knew the boys in my first novel, which I was writing at that time, weren't as raw as they could be, weren't *real*. I knew they were failing as characters because I wasn't pushing them to assume the reality that my real-life boys, Demond among them, experienced every day. I loved them too much: as an author, I was a benevolent God. I protected them from death, from drug addiction, from needlessly harsh sentences in jail for doing stupid, juvenile things like stealing four-wheel ATVs. All of the young Black men in my life, in my community, had been prey to these things in real life, and yet in the lives I imagined for them, I avoided the truth. I couldn't figure out how to love my characters less. How to look squarely at what was happening to the young Black people I knew in the South, and to write honestly about that. How to be an Old Testament God. To avoid all of this, I drank.

"I'll think about it," I said. I smiled. Demond smiled. The vein running down the center of his high forehead pulsed and the skin around his eyes bunched at the corners.

Rob put the last batch of the eighty pounds of crawfish to boil at midnight, cut the burner off, and then went inside and forgot about them, fell asleep. We all slept, drunk, lips tender, on sofas, on floors, in beds. I woke at 2:00 A.M. hungry and drunk and stumbled out onto the slab to find the pot cold, the crawfish bloated with water, soft and ruined, and rain falling, the drops fat and warm. The dominoes, the table, the chairs: all wet. When I stepped out into the grass, searching for some crawfish that had been spared, hidden away on a plate or container, the grass gave and my feet sank. Every step was an exercise in loss. I looked up into the rain, then gave up, slipped back inside, figured somebody would clean up the mess in the morning, and fell asleep in the bunk bed that my nephew slept in when he visited Nerissa.

ILLUSIONS WAS A club that had been many things before it became what it was for us that summer and the next. It had been a country bar, a teen club, a "Black" club, a pop club, and then finally it became what it would be when Katrina's storm surge bulldozed the beachfront property flat: a Black club we affectionally called "Delusions." The first floor consisted of a bar and small, crowded dance floor. Upstairs, there were pool tables, another bar, and a small space for a photographer to work, where my cousins and I took pictures in front of a banner spray-painted with a city skyline that was completely alien to the long, low towns of the Coast. God's Gift, the frame around the Polaroid reads. When the club was packed to capacity, the walls sweated and the glass fogged with perspiration.

That night, I drove to Illusions while Nerissa rode in the passenger seat and my brother's last girlfriend, Tasha, laughed in the back. We were perfumed, giddy, glad to be out of Nerissa's apartment, out of Demond's house, where we'd been spending a lot of time: *out.* I wore black. Rob and Demond followed in Demond's car, an older-model Z40 sportscar, sleek and low to the ground. My old boyfriend Brandon met us there. Charine and C. J. had decided to stay at Nerissa's apartment, watching *Forrest Gump* and smoking. Upstairs in Illusions, Rob gave us his shining grin, gold in his dark face, and bought Nerissa, Tasha, and me drinks. They were

walk-me-downs, fluorescent blue and sweet, made of nearly
every liquor behind the bar. I couldn't taste the alcohol in it.
I gulped mine down, anxious, almost, for the buzz to hit. We
stood at the end of the bar with Rob and Brandon, a cigar at
the corner of Rob's mouth, watching the women gliding like
sleek ducks through the crowd, dressed in gold and pastel
denim, hairstyles molded stiff, and the men separated by hood,
drinks in hand, stopping girls with a pinched waist, a grasped
wrist, a smile, *hey*. I looked at the crowd of people and wondered at their stories, and for a sober moment I knew that their
stories were ours, and ours theirs.

"Y'all want another one?" Demond asked. The corner of
his mouth made a gesture at a smile.

"Yeah," Nerissa said. I nodded, as did Tasha. He bought
us each another drink, slid them across the bar to us. The
clear plastic cups were cold to the touch, perspiring instantly.
I drank. When I swallowed, I smiled at Demond in what was
supposed to be an unspoken thank-you. Demond laughed
and told me that he liked my outfit. His dreadlocks swung.
He was handsome, fair, charming. Women approached him,
lingered in his field of vision, waiting for him to talk to them,
to hit on them, to say hello. He didn't have to flirt. People
were attracted to him, and he was charismatic enough to draw
them even closer to him with conversation when he wanted
to. When he didn't the planes of his face were more severe
and he was a closed door, his eyes peepholes viewed from the
wrong side, obscuring everything. He had a temper. But that
night he was all geniality.

I sucked up the drink: I was thirsty, and it was cold and
lemony. I danced at the bar. Nerissa threw her wrist over my

shoulder and danced with me. Tasha, who could dance better than both of us, laughed and drank. Everything turned hazy then: Demond's face blurred, and I told my sister I didn't feel so good. We went to the bathroom together. She took the last available stall, and I heard her vomiting into the toilet. I swayed and my throat burned. Something was wringing my insides out. I was wretched.

"Fuck it," I said, and leaned over the garbage can, large and full to the brim. I threw up. Everything was hot and sticky: I could feel the bass thudding through the building from the dance floor downstairs through the grimy tile of the bathroom wall. Pretty girls using napkins to wipe sweat from their foreheads: they walked in and out of the bathroom, ignoring me. Some girl in purple and gold stumbled in wearing stilettos and said, "Get it all out, baby." This was comforting, and I gurgled. Vomit splashed on the top layer of plastic cups. Nerissa came out of her stall, and suddenly I was finished. The world spun. I grabbed her shoulders, followed her out of the bathroom, and blacked out.

When I came to, I was in the backseat of my car, slumped over in the center. Nerissa was on my right, leaning over on my shoulder. Tasha's back was to me because her head rested on the upholstered seat. Brandon and Rob and Demond's voices were loud. I opened my eyes only long enough to see them standing near the two open doors of the car, smiling down at us. The breeze from the Gulf cut cleanly through the car, hot and salty. I couldn't move.

"Walk-me-down, huh? It sure walked them down," Brandon said.

"Look at them," Rob said.

We were all sick.

"It's not funny!" Tasha yelled, and in my drunken stupor, I felt like laughing. They did this: despite all, they made us laugh damn near every time we were together. But I couldn't open my mouth. I could only listen as Demond laughed for me, clean and cutting, and the wind carried it away across the parking lot to the Outback steakhouse, where it sputtered away like a desultory breeze. I curled in on myself. All I wanted in the world was for it to go dark, to not exist. I wanted to black out again. Then I did.

THE NEXT TIME we met at Illusions was New Year's Eve of 2004, over a year later, and there were more of us. This is when we took the picture with the God's Gift background. I left my hair down, curly and big, wore a red one-shoulder shirt and red boots with silver studs and silver stiletto heels shaped skinny and sharp as knives. In the picture, we are all drunk, and everyone smiles. We know that taking this cheap picture is tacky, but we are a neighborhood, a community, a hood, a family, so we grin. Knees bend, hips angle, waists are grabbed. Drunk and sentimental, I loved every one of them for still being alive.

I never drove home when I was drunk. One of my more sober cousins or friends, one of my sisters maybe, drove us back to DeLisle that night, where we ended up in Demond's yard at 4:00 A.M. The sky was deepest black, salted with stars. We were all drunk, all high, all smoking packs of Black & Mild cigars while we perched on car hoods. The music played in the cars where some of us sat having conversations, club-sweaty, intoxicated and serious. Demond wove his way through the cars with a 22-ounce of beer in his hand, talking and laughing.

"You on a all-night flight, huh?" he asked me as I leaned on the car next to my cousin Blake, passing a cigar back and forth, which I had never smoked before. It was so strong it was making me dizzy and tingly, and I liked the sensation, but not enough to smoke one again, I thought. It was making my throat burn.

The night pulsed with bugs; they gave low, staccato ticks. I smiled at Demond, at all of them. There was no place I wanted to be more than that yard, leaning on that car, interior lights flashing on and off, a lone streetlight a block away leaving us wide-eyed, struggling to see each other in the dark.

Demond ducked his head into the window of a car where two of my cousins were sitting and said, "Hey man, turn the music down." He didn't wait for them to reply and walked off, his dreads swinging. He liked the party, but he didn't want the county cops to wander by and stop, drawn by the music, and he didn't want the neighbors to complain. Not only did he have responsibilities, but he also had spent the last couple of years dodging the kind of bad luck that afflicts the innocent in drug-plagued neighborhoods, where every other cousin or friend is a drug dealer, every older cousin or friend an addict. Demond had been witness to the aftermath of a shooting and had agreed to testify against the alleged shooter. The shooting had occurred in DeLisle, during a holiday. He'd also agreed to testify against a drug dealer who wasn't from DeLisle but had been operating in the neighborhood. His conscience had made him agree to testify in the first case, and since he'd been stopped while riding in a car with the drug dealer in the second case, self-preservation had made him agree to testify in the second. These things weighed on him and he felt he had no room for error.

My cousins rolled their eyes, said "Fuck that nigga," and kept the volume where it was. The sun came up, washed the yard a milky gray, then white, and we departed one by one to our houses, where we eased open doors, tiptoed inside, and fell into dead sleeps while the sun burned its way higher into the sky and the community rose to face the day. Everything about the night seemed stolen, lived in those murky hours while others slept or worked. We crawled through time like roaches through the linings of walls, the neglected spaces and hours, foolishly happy that we were still alive even as we did everything to die.

On February 26, 2004, Demond was working third shift, at night. He called Rob before he left work, told him he would call him when he made it home, that maybe Rob could ride with him to a twenty-four-hour pharmacy in Gulfport, to Walmart, to get diapers for his daughter.

On another night, Demond would have driven to DeL-isle, turned into Rob's mother's driveway, which dipped down from St. Stephen's, and stopped to the side of Rob's mother's house. Rob would have loped out, slid into the passenger seat of the maroon two-door car, eased into conversation with Demond, and they would've driven up Lobouy Road, pine-cloaked under the night sky, thick with animal secrets, to the interstate. At that hour, Gulfport would have been desolate:

a stretch of chain stores, fast-food restaurants, two-story hotels, neon lights, black and yellow oil-spotted parking lots, and beyond them, pines and ranch-style houses divided into subdivisions. Demond's car would have been one of a few idling at stoplights, filling up in gas stations, parked near the doors at Walmart. They would have flicked the ashes from their cigars out the window to turn to dust on the asphalt. It would have been a night like any other, where the company of a friend eased Demond out of a shift spent standing, repetitively doing one thing or another. But this was not a night like any other night because Demond never showed up at Rob's house.

Later, talk around the factory where Demond worked, from the guard shack, would be that there was a truck lurking near the gates, that someone was watching the cars leave after second shift, arrive for third. Instead of going to Rob's after he left work, Demond went home. Rob waited for him and fell asleep. In Rob's blue room, the light from the television pulled him into his dreams: Rob slept, and the light shone over him with an aluminum crackle, flashing, but he didn't wake. Neither did anyone in the houses next to Demond's, or in the house across the street. Neither did Demond's fiancée or his daughter when someone stepped out of the bushes in front of Demond's house and shot him as he walked up to his door, tired and grimy with dried sweat, wanting a shower, maybe a beer. Hours later, Demond's absence in that cavernous room, in a cold bed, woke his fiancée. She looked outside and saw his car. She walked out on the porch, her small feet making the wood creak, and saw someone asleep on the lawn. Who was asleep in the yard?

Demond lay there, his dreads splayed away from his head, his face still, his eyes open, his chest red; but for that, he would have been asleep. She fell on him and screamed.

CHARINE GOT THE call at around seven o'clock the next morning. We had a de facto phone tree: the first person to hear would call the second person, who would call the third, who would call the fourth, and somewhere in that line someone would call Rob, who would call Nerissa, who would call Charine, who would tell me, no matter the time. I was home for my spring break, asleep, dreaming of nothing, when she came into my room in my mother's house, switched on the light, and without preamble said, "Mimi, Demond's been shot." I heard her, covered my eyes, breathed. Death rushed me like water does the first summer jumper into a still-chill spring river.

"What the fuck!" I said.

Charine hopped from one foot to another.

"What happened?" I said.

"I don't know. It might be drug-related. You know he was supposed to testify against that dude from New Orleans."

Charine climbed into the bed with me, turned toward the wall. If she cried, she was silent, and I could not feel it in her back or her stomach. I spooned her, threw my arm over her ribs, held her like I had when she was a baby, when she was growing out of her chubby precociousness to walk, and I was an eight-year-old growing faster from the legs than anywhere else. She fell asleep, and every time my arm rose and fell with her breath, I thanked something that she still breathed, even as I was sick about it, whatever it was, that killed us one after the other. *Senseless,* I thought. *This is never going to end,* I thought. *Never.*

I woke up four hours later. My eyes were puffy and red, matted at the seams from crying, from sleeping. I threw on a sweatshirt and drove with Charine to meet Nerissa at Demond's house. I played one song over and over in my car, parked on the street, felt the acute sense that life had promised me something when I was younger, that it wouldn't be this hard, perhaps, that my people wouldn't keep dying without end. *I'm only twenty-six,* I thought. *I'm tired of this shit.*

We sat with Demond's fiancée, a widow at my age, her face swollen, red-tinged underneath the black. She smoked cigarette after cigarette.

"I didn't hear anything," she said. "Nothing."

She said it as if the fact that she hadn't heard the gunshot meant it couldn't have happened. We did not know then that the police would conduct an investigation for a few months, post signs at the local gas stations near the interstate asking for any information about Demond's murder. We did not know the murderer would remain faceless, like the great wolf trackless in the swamp, and the police's search would be fruitless.

On the day after Demond died, I sat on his concrete porch steps. When the sun set, the coven of bats that lived in Demond's roof burst from the vents and out into the night in a black, squeaking mass. Where we had parked and drank and gotten high on Demond's lawn, now there was yellow police tape draped from pine to pine, circumventing the mimosa. It read: CAUTION. Nerissa smoked, exhaling clouds into the cold air, the skin dry at the sides of her mouth, and I wondered who had come out of the dark and killed Demond. Even as I knew the figure that had waited hidden for him in the shivering pockets of the trees was human, I wanted to turn to Nerissa and ask her: *What do you think it is? What?*

WE ARE WOUNDED
1984–1987

My mother, my father, Josh, Nerissa, and I moved from the small house in the big field to a cream and yellow single-wide trailer in DeLisle on a dead-end red-dirt road. The road was mostly wooded, but there was a cluster of houses near the dead end, and each of those houses contained boys whom I would be friends with for the rest of my life. I was seven then. Joshua and I and the boys spent our days swinging from my father's punching bag, which he'd hung from a pecan tree in the front yard, having mud fights, running races down the middle of the road, picking unripe pears by the wagonful from my aunt's house farther down the street and eating so many we grew sick. I thought my parents were mostly happy then, but now I know my own happiness blinded me.

One day my father came home with a motorcycle. It was a Kawasaki Ninja, new, red and black, glossy.

"Stay off of it," my father said. "You can't play on it."

"It's yours?" I asked.

"Yeah," my father said. Then he squatted next to me, pointed to the silver parts on the machine near the steel bars where he rested his feet, and said, "You see them things there?"

I nodded.

"They get so hot that they can burn you. That's why you can't play on it."

"Yes, sir," I said. My parents taught me and my siblings that we should address them that way, with polite deference, when they gave us commands.

My mother was quiet. She pushed her glasses, thick and wide in the style of the day, overpowering her small, beautiful face, up her nose. She sniffed, and a frown nicked the side of her mouth. She looked away and then walked back into the house, slamming the door. When we followed my father into the house after loitering around the bike, after watching my father rub it down with a cotton cloth, polish the metal, listening to the faint ticks the machine made as it cooled down, my mother was cooking. She said nothing to my father, but her back was a shut door. I was a child; there was much I did not know. I did not know my father had taken funds he'd been saving, at my mother's insistence, to buy land, and had purchased his motorcycle with them. I did not know that his own father, my grandfather Big Jerry, who had been quite a playboy in his day but a devout caretaker to his children, had told my father: *You can't ride a wife and three kids on a goddamn motorcycle.*

"Go take a bath," my mother told us. We went.

AFTER LITTLE MORE than a year, the neighbors we were renting the trailer from decided to rent it to their relative instead. We moved across DeLisle to live with my grandmother Dorothy. I was eight. This was the house my mother grew up in, the same house some of her siblings had been born in. It was long, finished with wood siding, and set low to the ground, elevated on two cinder blocks in the front and three in the back, as it was built on a hill. Originally it had had a sizeable living room, a narrow kitchen, a small dining room, a bathroom, and two bedrooms. After my grandfather left my grandmother for another woman, she raised the seven children they'd had together on her own. She added two large bedrooms and a bathroom to the house. She took what my grandfather left her with, and she built it into something more, and she survived.

This is a common refrain in my community, and more specifically in my family. I have always thought of my family as something of a matriarchy, since the women of my mother's side have held my nuclear family and my immediate family and my extended family together through so much. But our story is not special. Nor had it always been this way. It used to be that the Catholic Church was a strong presence in my community and divorce unheard of; men did not leave their women and shared children. But in my grandmother's generation, this changed. In the sixties, men and women began to divorce, and women who'd grown up with the expectation that they'd have partners to help them raise their children found themselves with none. They worked like men then, and raised their children the best they could, while their former husbands had relationships with other women and married them and then left them also, perhaps searching for a sense of freedom or a sense of power that being a Black man in the South denied them. If they were not called "sir" in public, at least they could be respected and feared and wanted by the women and children who loved them. They were devalued everywhere except in the home, and this is the place where they turned the paradigm on its head and devalued those in their thrall. The result of this, of course, was that the women who were so devalued had to be inhumanly strong and foster a sense of family alone. This is what my grandmother did.

When we moved into her house, every one of my mother's siblings, their children, and my own nuclear family lived there. There were thirteen of us: my four bachelor uncles, my two aunts, who each had one son at the time, my grandmother, my father, my mother, Nerissa, Joshua, and me. My uncles slept two to the two smaller bedrooms, and my grandmother kept the master bedroom in the back with the bathroom. My aunts slept in the other, larger, more recently added bedroom in the rear of the house; the room was so large there were two double beds there, so each aunt shared a bed with her child. My brother and I slept on bunk beds shoved into a corner of that room. I took the top bunk, and my brother took the bottom. My mother and father nailed a curtain over the dining room door, moved the dining table into storage, and moved their own double bed in, where they slept with Nerissa and, after she was born in 1985, Charine. For the next two years I would have most of the people I loved living in one house, which was mostly wonderful for us kids, and a horrible strain for all of the adults, driven as they were to my grandmother's house by Reagan's policies in the eighties, which undercut whatever shaky economic footing the poor had, and depressed the listless southern economy.

★   ★   ★

By the time we'd moved into that rambling, lopsided wooden house, I'd already fallen in love with reading. I think my love for books sprang from my need to escape the world I was born into, to slide into another where words were straightforward and honest, where there was clearly delineated good and evil, where I found girls who were strong and smart and creative and foolish enough to fight dragons, to run away from home to live in museums, to become child spies, to make new friends and build secret gardens. Perhaps it was easier for me to navigate that world than my home, where my parents were having heated, whispered arguments in the dining room turned bedroom, and my father was disappearing after those arguments for weeks at a time to live at his mother's house in Pass Christian before coming back to us. Perhaps it was easier for me to sink into those worlds than to navigate a world that would not explain anything to me, where I could not delineate good and bad. My grandmother worked ten-hour-long shifts at the plant. My mother had a job as a maid at a hotel. My father still worked at the glass plant, and when he was living with us, he would often disappear on his motorcycle. My youngest uncle was in high school, but the other uncles worked, as did my aunts. There was often only me, Josh, Aldon, who slept in one of the double beds in that back bedroom with his mother, and a lone uncle who was off for the day in the living room, watching a movie on PBS, one of the two channels we had. Sometimes my two aunts were in the kitchen, sweating over pots the size of my torso filled with bubbling beans, making biscuits for the family from scratch. "Go outside and play," we heard. So I put my books away for a moment and went outside to play with Joshua and Aldon.

I wanted to be my own heroine. Behind the houses in a row along Route 357, a forest stretched. I'd followed my older cousin Eddie back through those woods once to a barbed wire fence with signs posted intermittently along its length that read: DELISLE FOREST, PROPERTY OF DUPONT, NO TRESPASSING. This fenced property stretched from the Bay up behind our house, and then down all the way to my elementary school. Du Pont had put in a bid to build a factory in DeLisle in the seventies, promised lots of jobs to the community, and when approved, leased enough land for a plant but also enough to provide a buffer of woods between them and us. When I followed my cousin Eddie, who must have been twelve at the time, back to that fence, I watched him jump over it, a rifle in hand, and disappear into the dark. He was hunting rabbits, squirrel, anything wild and gamey that would yield a little meat after it fell to his bullet. Part of me wanted to go with him, the other was afraid. Those woods were lovely and menacing, all at once. And access to them was forbidden.

When I played with Joshua and Aldon, I wanted to lead them back into those woods, to explore them like the characters in *Bridge to Terabithia* did their forest, but I did not. Instead, Josh and Aldon and I wandered around the shed in the backyard, leapfrogging over the septic tank, sliding along the slippery slope where what had been an artesian well slowed to a slick trickle to create a bog in the middle of the yard. We explored behind my great-aunt's house. She lived next door. There we found a good plot of pines. Hidden beneath their shade was straw-strewn earth, and sticky stumps and trunks, brown and flaky, felled by hurricanes.

"We are going to have our own place," I said. "We need to come up with a name for it."

"What we going to name it?" Aldon asked.

I looked down at them both. They were five, three years younger, and shorter than me. Their big heads seemed too big for their shoulders, their hair was a fine dusting, and their eyes were wide. Joshua was bright-skinned and Aldon was darker, but both wore cropped satin and net shirts that looked like football jerseys and khaki shorts with nasty metal zippers that hurt my fingers whenever I helped one of them get dressed. They were depending on me. Where one went, the other followed, and right now they were both following me. We'd find our place, our own little world.

"Kidsland," I said. "We'll call it Kidsland."

"Kidsland?" Joshua asked. When he said it, it sounded like *kizzland*.

"Yeah, Kidsland, like *kid's . . . land*. Because it's our land. Our kingdom."

"Yeah, that's good," said Aldon.

"I like that," said Josh.

I led them out into the trees. Downed trunks became horses and castles. Branches became swords and enemies. We battled. We ran. Joshua collided with a tree and scraped himself purple. I clucked over it, wiped it clean with my shirt, blew on it.

"It hurts," he said.

"It's going to be okay," I told him.

Joshua trusted me. His eyes, which had glazed wet, dried. He shrugged, hopped a little on his good leg, ready for more serious play. I was proud of him.

I was still dissatisfied with the name. *It sounds so plain,* I thought, *not magical like Terabithia.* But I was happy with Kidsland, our home, with Aldon, with Josh. *Two good warriors,* I thought. I was a little satisfied, as if I'd taken the first step to doing something momentous, to becoming one of those girls in the books I read.

IN REAL LIFE, I looked at my father and mother and understood dimly that it was harder to be a girl, that boys had it easier. Here, boys could buy and ride motorcycles and come and leave when they wanted to and exude a kind of cool while they stood shirtless at the edge of the street, talking and laughing with one another, passing a beer around, smoking cigarettes. Meanwhile, the women I knew were working even when they weren't at work: cooking, washing loads of clothes, hanging them to dry, and cleaning the house. There was no time for them to just relax and be. Even then I dimly knew there was some gendered difference between my brother and me, knew that what the world expected of us and allowed us would differ. But for me, the reality of those differences was reduced to one tangible symbol: cigarettes.

I could read the packages, knew that my uncles smoked Kools. To me, they embodied just that, the leisure and cool that were the specific privilege of men. When Joshua and Aldon and my cousin Rhett and I collected enough loose change from the grown-ups, we'd jump on our bikes and ride them down the street, a mile or so, to a store built in a shed in a yard. The owners were White. I often felt like they were staring at us as we carefully picked our pack of gum, our potato chips, our one drink, our candy. Two dollars could buy us this, but if we had less, if we had only a dollar, our options were narrower. Joshua and Aldon would choose all candy, penny candy and Now and Laters, Rhett chips and drinks, and I'd buy candy and gum. My favorite candy was candy cigarettes. I'd smoke my candy cigarettes during the bike ride back to the house: my favorite brand had some sort of fine powder on the tip, so when I put my lips to the gummy candy filter and blew, a light smoke flew like sea spray.

One day, one of my uncles puffed his cigarette, sucked it down quickly, threw it down in the dirt with a quarter of it remaining, and then walked down the street. The porch was empty, my aunts in the house were quiet, and we were alone in the dirt yard. I slid under his car, plucked the cigarette from where he'd flicked it. It was still warm. I held it by the filter, the tip pointed to the ground, and walked over to Josh and Aldon.

"Come on, y'all," I said.

They stood and followed me around the back of the house. I stopped between the back wall of the house and the concrete slab of the septic tank.

"We're going to smoke this cigarette," I said. I wanted some of my uncle's autonomy, some of his freedom.

They nodded sagely, as only five-year-olds can do. I tried to puff the cigarette and got nothing. Before I could hand it to Aldon, Aldon's mother heard us from the bathroom window, which I'd parked us right beneath.

"Mimi, Aldon, Josh: get in here!" she yelled.

We dropped the cigarette and filed into the house. Both of my aunts sat at the kitchen table.

"What were y'all doing?"

I didn't say anything.

"Y'all were smoking a cigarette?"

"No," I said, suddenly panicky, my chest flushed hot.

"Don't lie," my other aunt said. "Was y'all trying to smoke a cigarette?"

"Yes," I said, miserable.

"I heard everything from the bathroom window," Aldon's mother said. "Why did y'all do it?"

"I don't know," I said. "I saw it and I picked it up."

"Well, don't ever do it again," she said. "Y'all don't need to smoke."

"If y'all promise not to ever do it again, we won't tell your mama."

"Okay." We all nodded.

They sent us back out to play. I was relieved, knowing that we'd escaped a terrible punishment. Later that night, as Mama was drying Joshua off after giving him a bath, he told her, "Mimi and Aldon were smoking a cigarette." My mother called me into the bathroom and confronted me. I told her what my aunts had said. She was angry they hadn't told her about our escapade. I wished my father were there, but he was out. My aunts told my mother the truth. My mother's work was never done. She whipped Joshua and me and punished us by confining us to our bunk beds in the back bedroom, dark as a cave in the middle of the summer, for a weekend. We came out to eat and use the bathroom. We slept and whispered to each other: I read, sometimes to him. While we suffered, Aldon giggled and played outside: our aunt was more lenient with him. Joshua and I watched his shadow waver across the screen, behind the curtains, with the pecan and pine trees. I was bitter: even in punishment, some boys had it easier.

BUT ON MOST Saturday mornings, we were free from adult worries. The house was ours, since we woke at 6:00 A.M. to sneak to the living room, where we turned on the TV for Saturday morning cartoons. We lay for hours on the living room floor, recently carpeted in dark blue, to watch the Smurfs, the Snorks, Tom and Jerry, the Ewoks, the Looney Tunes. Our favorite show was *Popeye*. They broadcast the show out of a studio in New Orleans: the Popeye's fast-food chain invited White kids to the studio to sit in bleachers to balance small, greasy cartons of fried chicken and biscuits on their laps while a host introduced all the cartoons. I was so hungry then my stomach burned and hurt in sharp, little pains.

"I'm going to make us something to eat," I said. Every Saturday, I scaled counters to reach in cabinets, took out the WIC-issued cornflakes and powdered milk. I mixed the powdered milk by the instructions in a half-gallon pitcher, fixed us all bowls of cereals that we ate standing in the doorway so we could watch cartoons and eat. We would be whipped if we ate and spilled anything in the living room. The cereal—no, the milk—didn't taste right. It didn't taste like the store-bought milk I remembered having before we moved to my grandmother's, when my father had a good job and could afford milk that came wet and cold in gallons. He'd lost his job at the glass plant after he mislabeled boxes, and was moving from job to job. Some Saturdays I added cups of sugar to the powdered milk because I thought it would make it taste like the real thing. It didn't, but at least it was sweet. Joshua and Aldon and Nerissa and I ate the clumpy, watery mess over our cornflakes, and we were still hungry. Every Saturday we stared at those fair-haired children on *Popeye*, healthy and plump and pink, who got to cup their hands to their eyes like binoculars and screech "Roll 'em!" before each cartoon while their laps turned splotchy from the grease leaking from their chicken boxes. We ate everything in our bowls, scraped the bottoms with our spoons, drank the last milky sugar from the bowl, and I, with the cereal disintegrating to silt in my spiteful stomach, hated them.

BETWEEN JOBS, MY father spent some time with us. *The Last Dragon* was my father's favorite movie, so we watched it over and over until we knew all the words. We acted it out in the dining room turned bedroom; he was Sho'nuff, Josh was Leroy Green, and I was Laura Charles. When my father was home, it seemed that my mother wasn't: I never saw them in the same room together. I knew something was wrong, but I could not articulate what it was. Sometimes my father strapped us to the back of his motorcycle, where my brother or I clung to his back like monkeys, and he rode us around DeLisle or Pass Christian, headphones smashed into our soft heads under the weight of the helmet. Prince's "Purple

Rain" blasted from the cassette player my father had strapped to his waist. Sometimes I think I should have known he was trying to tell me something, something like *I am a man, I am young and handsome and alive, and I want to be free*, but I did not. After a few weeks, my father got a job at an oyster factory in Pass Christian, which paid much less than the glass plant. On his hours off, he dressed in expensive leather riding suits he'd bought when he worked at the plant, combed his long black hair back into a braid, and rode the coast. What I did not know at the time was that he was riding to see his girlfriends, of which there were many, to strap them to the back of his motorcycle. I don't think he told them that he was married or had a family, and I don't know if he was thinking about them or us when he brought home five-gallon buckets of fresh oysters from his job still in the shell and stood out in the backyard shucking them. He still wore his long black rubber boots and work overalls, and ate the oysters raw while the sun set. Sheets, fresh on the line, billowed behind him.

"Can I have one?" I asked him.

"You're not going to like it," he said.

"I just want to try it."

"They're alive," he said, "when they go down."

"They see all the way down your throat?"

He nodded.

"You still want to try one?"

I wanted to do it because he said I couldn't. I wanted him to be proud of me. I wanted it to be the two of us standing in the yard, eating oysters in the dusk, always.

"Yeah."

He skewered the shell, popped it open with a flip of his wrist. The oyster meat was gray, streaked with silver, a purple trill at the center where my father cut it from the shell.

"Here," he said, holding the oyster out to me flat on the blade, as if it were a spoon. "Open your mouth."

I opened my mouth, sucked the oyster in. It was warm and salty and wet: I imagined it smothering in the pink insides of my mouth, staring at the dark tunnel of my throat in despair. I held it there, considering.

"Don't spit it out," my father said, and the burlap sack of oysters at his feet shifted, clinked. "Do not spit it out."

It was too warm. It was alive.

"Swallow."

I consigned the oyster to death and swallowed. My father looked pleased.

"You like it?"

I'd hated it. I shook my head. My father laughed, and his teeth were very white in his face, which became duskier and darker as the sun set. He stuck the knife in the seam of the oyster again, shucked again. He balanced the oyster delicately on the knife, brought the knife to his mouth, and sucked the oyster inside. I switched from foot to foot, scratching the inside of my calf with the thick skin on the bottom of my feet. I wondered how he never cut himself, how he could be so beautiful, so tall, so impressive.

ON MY EIGHTH birthday, I didn't have a party. The year before, my parents had thrown me an extravagant party at my grandmother's house, where all my cousins came to sing "Happy Birthday" to me over a large pastel sheet cake, and I'd worn a fancy purple and white dress, and been given a brand-new bicycle with a lavender banana seat. The following year, money was tight. On this birthday, my parents walked me out the door off the kitchen of my grandmother's house and unspooled a white and blue rope, thick as my neck, from the trunk of the family car. I was puzzled. My father laughed. The rope was long, twice as long as the driveway.

My father wrapped the rope around his shoulders and under his arms until he wore it like a great, thick coat, and then he climbed the live oak tree that shaded the side of the house and reached out its dark limbs over the roof. Once he reached the branch that overhung the roof, he inched his way along the limb until he was near the middle. He unspooled the rope and tied one end of it in a massive knot, which he tugged and tested until he was sure it wouldn't give. He tied the other end of the rope, tested that knot as well, before sliding down what was now a tall swing, at least thirty feet long, made of rope so thick a grown-up could sit on it and swing without a wooden seat and would still be comfortable.

"Happy birthday," my mother said. She put one hand on the back of my neck; her hand was rough from constant rubbing against sheets and bedspreads and towels and from the industrial-grade cleansers that the hotel housekeepers used. Years later, she would tell me that she was miserable at that job, that the work was hard and endless, that the women that she worked with gossiped about her and my father's relationship and were overtly mean and catty to her.

"Do you like it?" my mother said. Even at eight I knew she felt bad for not being able to give me more, for giving me, in its basic incarnation, a piece of rope for my birthday.

"I love it," I said, and I meant it. I sat in the seat and my father pushed me for a few minutes before going inside. Then I grabbed it in both hands and pulled my way up it, holding tight with my legs, struggling with my whole body, until I got to the top, where I touched the underside of the branch my father had straddled minutes before. I was high, at least thirty feet in the air, and my heart tripped. I looked out over the roof of the house, the yard, the next door neighbors' small maroon trailer, the street, the mysterious woods. I felt proud of myself for being able to climb, for being not afraid, so unafraid that I would spend hours during the summer and winter climbing the rope, gripping it with my thighs, and perching high on the swing, watching the world. And something about clinging to the top of that rope made me feel closer to my mother and father, even though, physically, I was as far away from my parents as I could get. Sometimes if I begged persistently and sweetly enough one of my uncles would pull the seat of the swing back, hold me above their heads, and let me go, and I would fly across the yard, white-knuckled as I gripped the swing, ecstatic.

MY PARENTS WERE trying to salvage their marriage. Sometimes on the weekends, my father and mother would make time for each other, and they'd leave us with one of their friends who lived in a cluster of apartment houses in the next town over. This friend babysat my brother and me often. From listening to adult conversation, I knew her husband beat her, and I knew that this was wrong. That was clearly delineated at least, and I knew this because once my mother's entire family rode to Pass Christian with shotguns when my aunt's boyfriend beat her: they stood out in the street in front of his house and told him if he ever touched her again, they would kill him, and he did not beat my aunt again.

Once, when I was nine and Joshua was six, my parents' friend dared Joshua to drink from a bottle of hot sauce, and my brother, who always had a stomach of iron and had eaten dog food once when I dared him, drank it.

"Your booty going to be burning when you doo-doo," she said.

He looked at her and smiled. His teeth were red. His breath was hot with Tabasco.

"No it's not," he piped up.

I was impressed. She tried to pass the bottle to me but I demurred. Sometimes he led and I followed. I realized that this time belonged to him. She made grilled cheese sandwiches for us and gave us small plastic cups of red Kool-Aid. My brother and I ate the sandwiches in big, breathless bites. Josh and I ran around barefoot in and out of the apartments, leaping from stairs, playing with stray cats, giving the Dumpsters in the parking lot a wide berth. They stank, and people sometimes missed the Dumpsters and left the garbage to rot next to them.

One day my parents' friend left us downstairs, watching TV, while she visited her upstairs neighbors.

I was distracted. Maybe I wanted another grilled cheese sandwich, so I ascended the stairs to find the door to their apartment open. Their apartment was mostly dark, and pieces of art made of stretched velvet and glass etched with colored veins that made the glass look marbled hung from the walls. The couple was a white couple, and my parents' friend and the man and woman sat in chairs around a smallish kitchen table. In the middle of the table, a mirror lay face up. The man was sliding a razor along the surface of the mirror, separating white powder into lines. He bent over and sniffed like he was sucking up his snot, like he was clearing his nose. His hair fell forward across his face. My parents' friend looked up and saw me standing in the doorway and said, "Mimi, go downstairs." I went. I did not know what it was. I did not know that I'd seen some of what grown-ups who were poor and felt cornered and at their wits' end did to feel less like themselves for a time. I did not know this need would follow my generation to adulthood too.

SOMEHOW MY MOTHER and father still scraped together enough for our Christmases. For days beforehand, my grandmother cooked, made big pots of seafood gumbo and homemade biscuits, pecan and sweet potato pies. The fire in the wood-burning stove in the living room ran so hot, the grownups went outside to feel the cool air and take turns pushing each other on my rope swing. My brother and I slept uneasily on Christmas Eve, Joshua because he was giddy about the prospect of presents, and me because I was nine and wanted a ten-speed with everything in me, and I was wondering if all the begging I'd done for one would pay off. If there would be a miracle. When I finally fell asleep, I dreamed the county police had come to the house to take all my uncles and my father away to jail. In my dream, I cried, and when I woke up, my face was wet. I do not know why I had that dream that night; I wasn't aware that my father or uncles were hustling or involved in criminal activities. Now, as an adult, I do not think they were. As an adult, I know they were men, rascals who loved to drink and smoke and raise hell on the weekends. But as a child, I listened to my grandmother when she worried about her sons, about them being stopped by the police and searched for no other reasons than they were Black and male, about them getting into fights with White men at bars and being arrested for assault while the White men they fought went free. And I saw the tight line of my mother's mouth when my father was absent and couldn't be accounted for, and heard her worry about him riding his motorcycle and getting into an accident and being taken to jail for it. To an impressionable nine-year-old, trouble for the Black men of my family meant police. It was easier and harder to be male; men were given more freedom but threatened with less freedom. But after I woke from that dream and woke Joshua, we crept into my parents' room to wake them and beg them to let us open presents, and a red ten-speed was propped in the corner of the living room for me, and I nearly forgot that dream.

★   ★   ★

My mother must have sat Joshua and me down and told us, perhaps in the living room on the same sofa where five years earlier my father had asked for my mother's hand in marriage. After having two children, my parents married; after having two more, they'd decided to divorce.

"Your daddy's not coming home. He's going away."

She didn't say *divorce*. We wouldn't have understood that word. But the next day, our father still had not come home from leaving for work the day before, and Joshua and I understood in our narrow, bony chests. Daddy was not coming home. He was going away. No more trailing around after him in the yard asking to hold nails or pieces of wood as he built rabbit hutches, no more fighting my way to the top of the rope swing, touching the branch, yelling "See!" to him, trying to make him proud.

Later, I would learn that my mother had said he should leave after she found out about his latest girlfriend, his youngest, the daughter of a coworker from the glass plant, who was fourteen when they met. She had worked a summer job at the plant the year that my father was fired. After my father lost his job and began working at the oyster plant and my mother found out about this latest infidelity, my mother realized my father would never change and their love was doomed. When my mother found out, she was pregnant with my fourth and last full sibling, Charine, but Joshua and I didn't know it yet.

After my mother told us this, I took to the room we shared with our aunts and curled in the bottom bunk, Joshua's bed, and alternately cried and read the latest book I'd checked out from the school library, shocked by the rejection of my father's leaving, which felt like a rejection not of his wife or his domestic life but of me. Children often blame themselves when a parent leaves, and I was no exception.

Joshua took to the yard. It was summer, and it was hot. He ran around the house, lap after lap, round after round, wailing, crying for Daddy. The uncles and aunts ran after him, caught him, held him squirming to them, told him to stop, but he sobbed louder and fought and squirmed in their arms. He was six now, longer, his once blond afro shaved short, and he was strong. They let him go and he hit the ground running and crying. He circled the house for hours, and he only stopped when he fell to his knees, his sobbing dying to hiccups and moans. He fell asleep like that, his head bowed, outside in the dirt. One of the uncles carried him inside, and I made room for him in his bed.

Soon after, my mother filed for Section 8, a government subsidy for housing, and found a house two towns over in Orange Grove, Mississippi, in a suburb going to seed, and told my grandmother we would be moving that summer. I turned ten. Before we left to set out on our own, and even though I suspected I was too old for it, I wandered around Kidsland again, tried to conjure some of the old magic, the belief, and could not.

THAT SUMMER BEFORE we moved, I hustled Aldon and Joshua and now Nerissa, old enough to sit still and pay attention, to the swing on the long concrete porch facing the road, and we played our favorite game: That's My Car. The rules were simple: as the oldest, I assigned each of us a number, and afterward, we sat and waited for our corresponding cars to drive by.

"I'm first and you're second." I put a calming hand on Nerissa, and she nodded.

"You're third."

"Okay," Aldon replied.

"And you're fourth," I told Josh.

The first car that passed the house from the direction of Du Pont, perhaps heading home from shift work, was dark blue, fairly new, and boxy.

"That's my car!" I yelled, and the others cheered.

A white two-door with a long, pointy hood zipped by.

"That's your car," I told Nerissa. We cheered dutifully. It was an okay draw.

We heard the next car before we saw it: a loud, syncopated clunking weighted by an ornery engine.

"Ooooooohhhhh," Josh crowed.

The car, gray and brown in patches, puttered across the street before us. The driver, as if he knew he drove a car he should be ashamed of, did not wave or blow his horn as a neighbor might, but instead looked straight ahead.

"That's your car!" I pointed at Aldon, laughing.

"Hunk of junk!" Josh screamed.

"Why I had to get the junky car?" Aldon said.

We all laughed. Aldon stood and waved his arms at the offending car as it chugged down the street, as if he imagined he could shoo it away as we did raccoons sniffing around the garbage or possums creeping with their pink feet through the fetid swamp of the backyard to disappear in the endless woods.

"Go! Go!" Aldon said, and we laughed harder. Nerissa clapped.

Aldon sat.

"Now it's Josh's turn," I said, and we faced forward on the swing, packed tightly one next to another, and watched the road. We listened intently for a whoosh, for a loud bang, for a flash of color, for anything that would signal our future.

CHARLES JOSEPH MARTIN

BORN: MAY 5, 1983
DIED: JANUARY 5, 2004

THE FIRST TIME C. J., one of my many cousins, moves into sharp relief is when he was around six and I was around twelve. He was fair and had a face full of freckles. As a toddler, he'd been blond like Josh, but as he grew older his hair darkened, grew long and curly, and his mother braided it to his head or cut it low on the top and left a long lock of it to grow down his back in a rattail. He was small and lean, angled all over with muscle. His face was shaped like a triangle, and the only things that were dark about him were his eyes, which were so deep in color they were a surprise.

At family reunions for my father's side, C. J. would be there, small and gold and wiry, his rattail touching him in the middle of his spine. We children ate hot dogs with ketchup and mustard, crunched potato chips, drank cold sodas in big gulps so that the fizzy acid burned our throats, and chased each other in packs around the yard.

"Flip," someone would say.

"Okay," C. J. said.

We lined up in a human corridor so he could showcase his skills. He jumped a couple of times and then ran headlong down the strip of grass we'd left. Near the end of the line he punched into a round-off, then a back handspring, and then another handspring, his rattail streaming out behind him. He was a human Slinky. We cheered. I felt hot and weak. Again and again he flipped down our aisle, hurling himself through the air, which was thick with humidity, and each time he cut it cleanly in two. When he landed on his feet, he bounced. When he grew tired, he'd run off to get a soda. The group would dissipate. I wandered off by myself, feeling dissatisfied with how earthbound my body was, how bound by the heat, until I wandered into a playhouse, a square of plywood and two-by-fours. Lying on the floor, sand scratching my back, I watched the other kids. They ran the yard in pairs, yanking at one another in the waning day, fighting for the last cold drinks. I watched C. J. dart between them, trip them, take what he wanted, and run away so quickly they couldn't catch him.

FOR A LONG time I did not see C. J. I went away to college when he was twelve, and when I came back, there he was: taller, my height at least, but short for a man. He was shirtless. The little-boy body he'd had was now larger, but he was still wiry, and his muscles were like rocks under his skin. There was no fat on him. He had grown all of his hair long and braided it back to his head, so his face stood out in hard relief. He was pale, freckled, and still able to do things with his body I could not imagine possible.

At this point, most of us lived with our parents, and while some of us had parents who didn't care if we had people over, others had parents who did (like my mother). And even most of the parents who didn't mind company minded if company came over too often, if there were lots of cars parked in the yard, because that attracted something we called *heat*: police attention. While that might not matter in neighborhoods that were mostly White and working-class, in our Black working-class community, it mattered. So kids from their preteens to their twenties spent most of their time down at the park, a former field that sat between the priests' rectory and the graveyard. The county hadn't invested much into its construction: they poured a small basketball court, then put up two swing sets, a wooden jungle gym, and two sets of small wooden bleachers that quickly rotted in the humidity and heat. My mother called the park "pitiful." It made her angry that our county park was markedly different from those in other towns in neighborhoods across the coast that were White or more moneyed. But we didn't care; we avoided the rotten spots on the bleachers and watched kids closely when they played on the jungle gym, and spent hours there, studiously ignoring the county police as they circled us like vultures, suspecting us of using and selling drugs wherever we gathered.

The day I took pictures of C. J. at the park, he wasn't in the game. We sat on the benches, watching some boys from the neighborhood play basketball on one of the four hoops.

Some of them were shirtless, sweat-glazed and shiny, others not, the cotton pasted to their chests before pulling loose at the neck and stomach. That day C. J. sat at the foot of the bleachers, smoking. Charine waited near him, a basketball in hand. She was around fourteen then. Every few minutes he'd walk up to Charine, and she'd throw the ball to him, and he would toss it in the air toward the hoop closest to the bleachers. Charine took a jump shot and missed it. The day was hot, heavy, and overcast, the rain perpetually five minutes away. The wind moved, and for a second it was cool. A tall Spanish oak tree shaded the bleachers where I sat beneath its green canopy, slapping mosquitoes dead. The road glittered in the distance.

Cars had pulled onto the grass near the basketball court, parked next to the concrete benches. Typically, boys who did this opened their doors and trunks and played music on loud audio systems.

Charine shot the ball, attempting jumpers and fade-away shots at the hoop closest to the fence near the Catholic priests' house. C. J. snatched the rebounds and ran for another basket, dribbling the ball hard and fast, picking up speed before throwing his body upward and through the air. The ball slammed against the backboard and then ricocheted out of his hand and flew back into the game at the opposite end of the court. C. J. flew so high that he dangled from the rim by the crook of his elbow, giggling madly, swinging slowly from side to side.

"Jesus," I said. I'd never seen someone so short jump so high. I cradled my old manual Nikon camera, hefted its solid weight, and yelled, "Do it again, C. J.!"

He dropped from the goal and bounced. Charine passed him the ball. He sprinted to the other end of the court and ran at his goal again, threw himself up in the air. He flew. Again the ball smacked into the wrong spot on the backboard, rebounded off, and again Charine caught it and threw it back to C. J. I walked down the bleachers, stood closer to the hoop, and tried to snap pictures of him, of the miracle of him flying through the air. But he was too fast and my camera was too old. I could hear the shutter snap open, lick against metal, and then snap shut again. Too slow. Later, when I developed that film back at college, C. J. would look all wrong in the air: awkwardly bent, blurry, all his terrific grace lost in the frozen moment captured by the camera.

"I can't do it, Mimi," C. J. said, walking to the bleachers. He said *Mimi* but it swung off his tongue before jerking short: it sounded like *May-me*. He and his closest cousin on Daddy's side of the family, Mario, were the only two people who said my name like that. "I can't." He laughed, shook his head, sweat streaming down his face, his hair turning wiry and golden at the root, giving him the blond halo Joshua'd had when we were children.

"Shit, you jump high enough," I said.

"You got it?" he asked, motioning toward the camera.

"I hope," I said.

C. J. WAS FOURTEEN when he and Charine began dating. He charmed her into it. There was something physically appealing in him: he was so short, so thinly muscled, his body performed magic for him. She and C. J. felt physically well matched, like a team. They didn't endure the lopsidedness that gendered differences in size and muscle could foster. They were cousins, which means many people, including some of our aunts, his mother, and my mother, hated that they were dating. But Charine didn't care, and neither did C. J. Cousins dated, had children, and married all the time in DeLisle and Pass Christian. They had for generations. In such small towns, in communities confined by race and class, this was inevitable. Charine loved C. J., and that's what mattered above all else.

From the beginning, Charine and C. J. were inseparable, which was only possible because C. J. was a nomad. He had a room with a twin bed in his mother's house in Pass Christian, but he rarely stayed there. Part of the roof and the ceiling in his room were caved in, and the floor and bed were covered in boxes of things that weren't his. When he was home, C. J. slept in the back living room. This room held a sofa and a little TV. He folded his clothes and stacked them on the back of the sofa, the television. He put small pictures, photos Charine took from me when I developed my film, of him and Charine and his cousins, on a side table. The door into the room was open to the kitchen and the rest of the house. His mother was a single mother to two children, C. J. and his much younger sister, and had never married either of their fathers. She worked hard to provide a home for her children, pushing against all the constraints and limitations of who she was and where she lived. Perhaps C. J. felt like he was a burden; perhaps this is why he spent months living in other places, sleeping on other couches.

When he wasn't living with his mother, he would sometimes live with his father in DeLisle, along with his father's girlfriend and her daughters. His father tried to integrate C. J. into his new family, gave him a car, worked on it with him to get it running, but it was never fixed. When he wasn't living with his father or his mother, he slept at our cousin Duck's house, who was Joshua's best friend. He slept in Duck's room, at the front of the house; Duck's mother didn't mind him staying there because C. J. was family. Children moved from family to family in DeLisle and Pass Christian through the decades: women in my great-grandmother's generation would sometimes give newborn children to childless couples after having five or ten or fourteen, and when children were older, they would often move out of the family home and live with different relatives. Sometimes they were driven away by their parents, and other times they were touched by the urge to wander. Here, family has always been a mutable concept. Sometimes it encompasses an entire community, which meant that C. J. also slept on the sofa in Rob's living room and the sofa in Pot's living room, though he was not related to them. At Duck's house, C. J. wore the same clothes for a few days in a row, and sat sleepily picking out his braids in the middle, hottest part of the day on the roots of an ancient oak tree at the corner of Hill Road and St. Stephen's. It was common knowledge that he was sitting on those massive roots waiting for his small clientele to show up so he could sell them drugs. I, like many others in the neighborhood, judged him for it. What I did not know at the time was that he hated sitting on that tree, that he wanted more for himself, but he didn't know how to get it.

When C. J. was seventeen, he dropped out of high school. School had bored and frustrated him simultaneously, and he left after ninth grade. I do not know exactly why, but I can imagine that he felt ignored and unremarkable in the classroom, yet another body crowding the school. He was not an academic standout, and he didn't like playing organized sports, even though he had the physical talent for it. The fact that he was a Black male barely scraping by in his classes meant he was seen as a problem. And the school administration at the time solved the problem of the Black male by practicing a kind of benign neglect. Years later, that benign neglect would turn malignant and would involve illegal strip searches of middle schoolers accused of drug dealing, typing these same students as troublemakers, laying a thick paper trail of imagined or real discipline offenses, and once the paper trail grew thick enough, kicking out the students who endangered the blue-ribbon rating with lackluster grades and test scores.

Sometimes C. J. followed Charine to Gulfport and stayed with her at my father's rented house in Gaston Point. C. J. and Charine wandered the streets of Gaston Point wearing basketball shorts and white wifebeaters under long white T-shirts. Both of them dressed like boys. They walked to the stores for bread, for milk, for lunch meat before returning to my father's house. They ate, watching movies and hiding from the heat. Sometimes in the cooler evening, C. J. would lift weights on the rickety weight bench my father had erected in the front yard.

On one particular hot summer day, one in a seemingly endless procession, C. J. and Charine and our cousin walked to the store for ice and Popsicles. On their way back, they heard a bark: breathy, tiny.

"You heard that?" Charine said.

"There," C. J. said, and pointed at the porch of a house they were passing, which was bordered by an aluminum fence.

"Y'all want it?" our cousin asked.

On the narrow, open porch of the house, a pit bull puppy sat, ears wide and soft as houseplant leaves, her feet the biggest thing on her. She scooted across the porch toward them, barking again, throwing her head up in the air with each sound, as if she had to use her full weight to toss it out. She was feisty. They liked her.

"Come on," C. J. said, and he vaulted over the low fence, scooped up the puppy, and carried her back to Charine, who opened her neon orange book bag and let them slide the puppy inside next to the Popsicles. They ran back to my father's rental house and unpacked the dog instead of groceries.

"It was ours," Charine said later. "It was like our baby."

WHEN I CAME home from Michigan during summers and winter breaks, I corralled Charine into spending time with me. Charine was the last of my mother's children who still lived in her house, so even though she was eight years younger than me, I made her my best friend. She usually invited C. J. along, and then we usually picked up two or three people from the neighborhood. I dragged them to the movies, paid their way, made them watch things like *Lord of the Rings,* and then afterward we'd all sneak into another movie, leaving the theater four hours after we entered it, queasy with buttered popcorn. On Fridays and Saturdays, we went out to Illusions.

In summer 2003, we piled into my car, Charine and Nerissa and C. J. and me, and met up with Nerissa's friend at a
hotel on the beach near Illusions. He'd been renting a suite
for a week. We had no idea why he'd been renting such an
expensive suite for so long, since he had a house: I assumed
he rented it because he could, because he wanted to brag
about his wealth, which he'd gained by selling dope. It was
an unspoken display of his status. Once there, we sat in my
car and got high. The Gulf water, black in the night, rolled
inexorably in. We felt good. We watched the parking lot of
the nightclub, the cars moving like a current past one another,
people swarming, preening. The bass from the club called
out, and the bass from the cars answered. When we went into
the hotel room, C. J. sat on the sofa. Charine sat on one of
C. J.'s legs, and I sat on his other leg. I'd never sat on C. J.'s
lap before: even in rest, his muscles were hard, and suddenly I
felt bad for sitting on him, for bearing down on his small
frame with my weight, so I stood.

"You ain't got to move," C. J. said. I sat back down. We
were quiet. We watched the TV without any sound and
watched Nerissa's friend, who'd been a top college football
draft pick but never gone to university. He walked to the
bathroom, where he stayed for a few minutes, and eventually
he emerged. He sniffed and sucked snot from his nasal cavity.
After swallowing, he'd laugh and talk with us. His sniffing
was staccato and annoying. *He stays with a sinus infection,* I
thought naively. He was restless, walking back and forth,
again and again.

"I have to go to the bathroom," I said.

There were cigarette butts in the sink and in the toilet. There was no toilet paper. There was no soap, and there was only one towel in the room; it lay on the floor, rumpled and dirtied. I decided I didn't need to pee, and went back to the sofa and sat next to C. J. and Charine.

"That bathroom is awful," I said, suddenly depressed.

"Come on," C. J. said, and we left the hotel room, darting between the cars speeding past on Highway 90 to the beach. The moon shone like a bleached oyster shell, and we spent the rest of the night until just before dawn drinking beer on the boardwalk. On the drive home, C. J., who was the only sober one, said, "They was doing coke in the bathroom."

"What?" I said.

"That's what they look like when people do coke in them. All them cigarette butts and shit."

I laid my head down on the seat, stared out at the thin white line of the beach, the trees, the water, all of it lightening from black to gray to blue. Eventually I fell asleep, thinking about what he'd said. Had C. J. been in another bathroom like that? How did he know? If C. J. said anything else, I didn't hear it.

WEEKS LATER, ONE night when my mother wasn't home, Nerissa and Charine and I sat at my mom's house, watching movies. The front door was open: the light was on. Charine left us to use the phone, and a few minutes later we heard a dragging noise scratching its way up through the darkness near the road and bordering woods, past the front yard.

"What the hell is that?" Nerissa said.

Charine ran out the front door, down the concrete front steps, and out to the road, where the dragging continued between pauses. Nerissa and I stood on the steps and saw C. J. and Duck standing at the edge of the pebbled drive. We walked down the driveway into the night to greet them. A blue ice chest with a long white handle sat between the boys, and C. J. sat down on it and turned up a can of beer. He offered us some. I took one and drank in sips, the beer bitter. Duck told jokes but didn't laugh at them. Duck didn't stay long. He left C. J. and us to the cooler. C. J. knew my mother disliked him, so he often kept some distance from my mother's house. For Charine and him, knowing that their relationship was opposed by so many lent it a romantic air, made them feel like star-crossed lovers. Even though Charine had told C. J. my mother was gone, we sat on the ground at the edge of the yard, slapping at mosquitoes and gnats, talking.

"Y'all can have this." Tipsy, I stood up. I was tired of the sharp bite and the itchy burn of the mosquitoes. "I'm going inside."

"Me too," Nerissa said. She followed me into the house. Charine remained outside with C. J. Twenty minutes later, the house phone rang.

"Hello?"

"Man, y'all come outside."

"Who this?"

"Your sister is upset. She think y'all mad at her. You need to come talk to her."

"Oh Lord."

Nerissa shrugged and kept watching TV. I walked outside, wondering what had gone wrong in the twenty minutes we'd been watching TV. C. J. pocketed his cell phone when I walked up. Charine was sitting on one of the wooden railroad ties my mother had used to landscape the yard. She was slumped over, and her face was in her hands.

"Your sister's crying," C. J. said.

"What for?" I said.

"She thinks y'all are disappointed in her."

"Where did this come from?"

"For real man, y'all sister love y'all."

I paused and scratched at my leg. I had no idea why Charine was so emotional, but I mistakenly understood it as hormonal histrionics: a teenage temper tantrum. She and C. J. must have gotten into a fight and she was funneling it into her relationship with me and Nerissa. The last place I wanted to be was outside in the yard with my needy sister. Regardless of how drunk or high he was, C. J. would choose to be no other place.

"I don't know what to say to her," I said. C. J. looked at me, his eyes wide and brown in the near darkness.

"Just talk to her," he said.

Charine wouldn't uncover her face.

"Charine." Her shoulders shuddered. "What's wrong?"

"Talk to her," C. J. said.

"I be fucking up," Charine said through her fingers.

"No, you don't," I said. "Calm down."

"Tell her you love her," C. J. said. He bent to the cooler, grabbed another beer, popped the top.

"What?" I said. "I'm talking to her."

"Tell her."

"Charine," I said. "I love you."

She cried harder. C. J. grabbed my arm and walked me off into the darkness, to the pebbled edge of the road. He leaned in to whisper, and his face was the brightest thing, made even harder than it already was by the night, which whittled his nose to nothing, his cheekbones to peach pits, his forehead, a sliver of light. He took a sip of his beer.

"For real, y'all don't understand. You need to talk to your sister."

He was insistent. I leaned away from the feeling that he held me by the back of my neck, like my mother had when I was a child and she led me through crowds by grabbing hard and bearing down.

"I'm going inside," I said.

"You should talk to her," C. J. said.

"All right," I said as I turned and glanced at Charine. She still sat on the crosstie, still hid her face, crying.

"I'll be inside," I told her, and then I turned my back on both of them and walked up the driveway. The woods were riotous with night bugs. C. J. tossed a can into the street. It clinked, then went silent. The rocks dug into my bare feet, but once I was a few feet up the driveway, I ran on my toes to lessen the bruise. *What the hell is wrong with them?* I thought. Charine's behavior I accredited to grief: Joshua had died three days before her birthday, and as the summer burned itself away to autumn, our loss made us act out in strange ways. I wondered to myself, *Is C. J. on something?* In the house, Nerissa was asleep; the TV turned her face blue. I heard shouting and the sound of the cooler being dragged, stopped,

then dragged again, so I knelt on the rough green trailer carpet and raised the blinds so I could look out the window. In
the pale reach of the one streetlight, C. J. tugged the cooler
a few feet, drank his beer, raised it to the sky, and yelled at
the woods. I couldn't hear what he was saying. He flung beer
after beer into the ditch, into the trees, kicked the cooler.
Charine followed him, sitting on the ground or the plastic
top of the cooler, or standing at his side. I could tell by the
way he slung the cans, which must have been half full because they flew far and fell quickly and didn't float like empty
aluminum, that he was cursing. I sank into the carpet,
watched Nerissa sleep, and wondered why I felt afraid.

"CALL EVERYBODY," I said. "We're going to New Orleans."

We left around 8:00 or 9:00 P.M. in a caravan, at least fifteen of us piled into a Suburban. None of us wore seatbelts. I
was stupid and didn't care. Ever since I'd left home, I'd learned
that life for me in the wide curious world was a constant
struggle against empty rooms, against the grief at my brother's death and at Ronald's death that followed me always,
that made itself most felt in those quiet spaces. When I was in
DeLisle, I liked to get as many of us as I could together,
cousins and hood, and organize trips to New Orleans, twenty
of us roaming Bourbon Street with Styrofoam cups. We
parked on Decatur Street and walked into the quarter. A
limousine with spinning rims was parked at the edge of the
lot; we noticed because these types of rims were new and
we'd only seen them on television. C. J. knelt next to the tire.

"Watch this shit," he said. He spun the wheel and the metal caught the light like a knife flipping through the air. "It's spinning!" he called. We laughed at the boldness of it, the silliness of it, the feeling that we were doing something stupid that we probably shouldn't be doing. We spent the night getting drunker and drunker, walking, eyeing the doors of strip clubs that only a few of us were old enough to enter. C. J. shepherded Charine through the drunk crowd the entire night, her protector; he was only an inch or two taller than she was, and just as lean, but when he walked next to her he seemed larger, bolstered by attitude, possessiveness, loyalty.

The next morning, I woke up on the daybed in the second bedroom in Nerissa's apartment. I stood up and walked toward the door, but my legs crumpled under me. I fell to the floor. I'd had fun the night before, and figured the only reason I felt so weak and had almost fainted was because of the migraine medicine I was taking to treat the headaches I'd suffered from since I was fifteen. C. J. and Charine and Nerissa and Hilton walked into the bedroom, and C. J. sat in a toddler's chair on the floor, a white T-shirt wrapped around his head, and looked at me.

"You ready to go at it again?" he said.

I smiled.

"Yep."

It was 8:00 A.M. We drank. We got high. C. J. plugged a small portable radio into the wall in the room with the daybed and the bunk bed, and he popped in a new Lil Boosie CD. He played the same song repeatedly; he rewound it over and over again and sang along. I'd never heard him sing before. His solid voice was clear through the T-shirt. He made me laugh with silly, unselfconscious jokes. He surprised me: I'd never known he could be so funny, so kind. And then, suddenly, the conversations shifted. We were talking about cocaine.

"You ever did it?" C. J. said.

"No," I said.

"You know anybody who did it? In college?"

"Yeah, a few people. But we weren't close."

"Don't never do it."

C. J. shifted in the toddler's chair he'd folded himself into, readjusted the T-shirt across his face, but it was too bulky and slid down. He was half smiling, half not.

"I tried it once," he said. "I did it again." C. J. rubbed his head. "I wish I'd never did it the first time."

I nodded and understood why he'd known the bathroom at the hotel was so disgusting, why he was so insistent and erratic that night he dragged the cooler up the road, why one day he'd scare me, and the next, he could be another person, kind and funny, painfully honest, telling me things he was somewhat ashamed to tell me while wearing a T-shirt like a veil across his face.

I GOT A feeling I ain't going to be here long, C. J. said. He told Charine this. He told his close cousins this. *Not here,* he said. He lived as if he believed it. He never talked like the rest of us, never laid claim to a dream job. He never said: *I want to be a firefighter.* Never: *I want to be a welder.* Neither: *Work offshore.* The only person he ever spoke to about his future was Charine; once every so often, he'd tell her he wanted her to have his children. *We can hustle,* he'd say, *make money. Live good,* he said. *Live.* But even after dropping out, he never got a legitimate job, perhaps dissuaded by the experiences of the young men in the neighborhood, most of whom worked until they were fired or quit because minimum wage came too slowly and disappeared too quickly. They sold dope between jobs until they could find more work as a convenience store clerk or a janitor or a landscaper. This was like walking into a storm surge: a cycle of futility. Maybe he looked at those who still lived and those who'd died, and didn't see much difference between the two; pinioned beneath poverty and history and racism, we were all dying inside. Maybe in his low moments, when he was coming down off the coke, he saw no American dream, no fairy-tale ending, no hope. Maybe in his high moments, he didn't either. *Don't say that shit,* Charine would tell C. J. when he spoke of dying young. *You ain't going nowhere.*

Years later, Nerissa told me a story she heard from one of C. J.'s friends in Pass Christian. They were walking along the train tracks, Nerissa said, because it was the fastest way to get around town. C. J. would have been surefooted, stepped easily over the hunks of granite that shifted while he skimmed from wooden crosstie to wooden crosstie. Over years, these had been burned black by the Mississippi sun and the heat of the trains. On either side of the tracks, ditches ran deep with water. Cattails grew tall. C. J. would have heard it first, the way the train whistled in the distance behind him. His friend loped on for a few steps and then crossed over the steel rails before wondering why C. J. kept walking, a small smile on his face, but even that was like a slide of rocks down a hill: all hard. Or perhaps C. J. glared at the ground when he walked. Either way, he ignored the blasting train advancing toward him. He ignored his friend, who flinched at the train's blast. *I ain't,* C. J. told people, *I ain't long for this world.* He waited until he felt the train cleave the air at his back, until the horn made his eardrums pulse, until he was sure the conductor was panicking, and then he called on his lean golden body to do what it would, and he jumped from the tracks, out of the way, alive another day.

C. J., HILTON, AND I spent January 4, 2004, at the park in DeLisle on the warped bleachers. C. J.'d asked Hilton to roll a blunt with some weed my sister gave him: the buds were bright green and damp and tight. C. J.'s blond-brown braids hung over his forehead and he smiled. The mild Mississippi winter sun made his blond eyelashes sparkle like gold wire. C. J. was mellow and calm. I asked him if he wanted to ride to the movies with us later that night and see Tom Cruise in *The Last Samurai.*

"For sure," he said.

As Hilton rolled the blunt, I watched cars pass by, and tried to persuade C. J. to light a fire in the rusty steel barrel used as a garbage can, to drive away the gnats.

"Come on, C. J. You know you want to light a fire."

"I think you want to do it, Pocahontas," he said to me.

"No, I don't. I protect nature." I laughed.

"Come on, Mimi. You can do it," C. J. said.

Hilton laughed at me; his face dimpled and his wide shoulders shook. I was depressed and hungover. I was dreading the drive back to Michigan the next day, its endless winter. I scanned the ground and assessed what I could use to set a fire: overgrown, dry winter grass, shorn oak branches, brown leaves, acorns, bits of napkins and potato chip bags and empty soda bottles littering the park. Through gaps in the pines, I saw two crackheads, our older cousins, former friends, walking up and down out on the main, pebbly street, waiting for dealers.

"I'm a junkie for this shit." C. J. laughed and held up the blunt. "Really, though."

I waved it away when Hilton offered it to me. They smoked for three hours until the sun set and a heavy fog rolled in with the night. Once every few years, a whiteout fog blanketed the entire Gulf Coast for days, reducing visibility to nothing. During winter fogs like this, we cursed and fiddled with our headlights, which did little to reveal the Mississippi landscape: our lights solitary seekers in the country dark.

We didn't end up going to the movies. I had to pack. I folded clothes and burned CDs for my sisters and my cousins and loaded my car and stood in my yard and listened to the cacophony, even in winter, of insects in the woods surrounding my house. It was a blessed noise to hear the sounds of home even if I couldn't see much of it in the thick fog. While I worked, Charine sat in my car in the driveway with C. J. and smoked for an hour or so. He didn't want to go to whatever his temporary home for the night was, to walk to Duck's house or Rob's house or Pot's house and sleep on the couch. He wanted to stay in my car with Charine, to talk into the night and through the morning. She was his home. But Charine told him: *I hate the cold.* She came inside around midnight, and he left. He walked down the street to Duck's house, disappearing into the fog. I imagine him standing beneath the big oak tree, waiting for his cousins to appear out of the fog and pick him up. If he couldn't be with Charine, he would avoid sleeping altogether and find other things to do with his night. They were planning to ride upcountry to bring his cousin's infant son home.

Charine had fallen asleep but I was still busy packing when the phone rang at two o'clock in the morning. It was C. J.'s mother. *Why is she calling the house?* I thought.

"Hello?"

"C. J.'s been in an accident—"

I thought: *No.*

"—and he didn't make it. Please tell Charine."

I thought: *I cannot do this.*

"Okay," I said.

C. J.'s mother sobbed and hung up the phone. I stared at the living room wall. I slumped over the sofa and tried to breath. The air felt wrong rushing down my throat. I called Hilton.

"Hello?"

I told him what C. J.'s mother had told me. I wiped my nose and said it all in a whisper.

"I cannot do this to her," I cried. "I cannot tell her this. I cannot wake her up and do this to her."

"I'm coming," he said.

Thirty minutes later I let Hilton in the front door. He walked past me through the living room into the kitchen into the den and into Charine's room. He switched on the light and shook her awake. He told her. She walked outside in the fog, and I put on my shoes. We three rode down to the park where I had seen him twelve hours earlier. We parked in the dark and people materialized out of the fog and woods and gathered with us until the sun rose, brought together again by a third tragedy, by another death and more loss and grief. They passed around blunts like napkins. My sister smoked until her eyes closed from the tears.

C. J. had ridden upcountry with his cousins: after they dropped the baby off, they hit a train. There was no reflective gate arm at the railroad crossing. There were flashing lights and bells that should have warned of the passing train, but they didn't consistently work, and because it was located at a crossing out in the county in a mainly Black area, no one really cared about fixing them or installing a reflective gate arm. On that night, even if the warning system had been working, that errant mechanical sentry at that lonely Mississippi county crossing, it was no match for that blinding winter fog. C. J. was in the passenger's seat. Our cousin swerved and slammed into the train with the right side of the car, which was crushed by the impact of the train car. C. J. was stuck in the automobile. The cousins tried to pull him out but he was sandwiched there. The car caught on fire and he burned while they stood by helpless, hollering for help into the cold white night, their cries swallowed by the Mississippi fog.

★   ★   ★

I CANNOT ASK Charine about the facts of C. J.'s death. There are things that I don't want her to think about, so I don't ask her if he was still alive after the car hit the train. I don't ask her if he spoke to his cousins when they tried to pull him from the car. I don't ask her if he was still conscious when the fire sparked. I cannot ask if that's what killed him, the fire. But I have heard stories from others, and they say he was alive. Some stories even say that he told them to leave him in the car while they were trying to pull him out; when I hear this, I think that he must have been in so much pain, his legs crushed by the metal, that he saw how futile their effort was. Some stories even say that the car burned and he was alive, and what is unspoken is that C. J. added his cries to his cousins' hollering for help and they all screamed there besides those faulty lights and the train track that cut through the woods. But I do not tell Charine these stories; I would not add to her burden of loss, especially when she already carries blame. Often she says that if she had sat a while longer in my car, if only, he would have stayed at our house with her instead of leaving and riding with his cousins upcountry. *If I would have stayed in the car,* she says, *he'd still be alive.* The burden of regret weighs heavily. It is relentless.

THE DAY AFTER C. J. died, we drove to our friend's house down the street, where we found him and four other boys from the hood sitting in a running car parked in his dirt driveway, beers in hand. They stared forward as if any minute they might hit the gas, drive north straight through the house, and leave this place. They cried with set faces. Charine climbed into the car, sandwiched in, and hugged one of them. I turned my back to the humming vehicle and covered my face. I saw everything. I understood nothing.

The night after C. J.'s death, I drove my sister around DeLisle while she smoked the rest of that batch of weed she had given C. J. We drove my tank dry into the morning as she rolled blunts, and I wondered if we were courting death: If we weren't, why did he keep following us, insistently, persistently, pulling us to him one by one? She smoked that bag, and after she finished it, she smoked through other bags. She told me they calmed her like cigarettes. She smoked every day, and for years after that night, she wept abruptly in the car without warning. When she did I turned the music up, and I let her cry, able only to say: "I know, I know."

I pride myself on knowing words, on figuring out how to use them so they work for me. But years later, my sister digs up C. J.'s funeral announcements, a pamphlet and a bookmark, after I ask her to do so. She begins crying, talks of regret and loss, grief constant as a twin, of how she dreams of C. J., and in every dream she is always chasing him. In those dreams, he is agile and golden as he flips and flies and leaps, and he will not allow himself to be caught.

The land that the community park is built on, I recently learned, is designated to be used as burial sites so the graveyard can expand as we die; one day our graves will swallow up our playground. Where we live becomes where we sleep. Could anything we do make that accretion of graves a little slower? Our waking moments a little longer? The grief we bear, along with all the other burdens of our lives, all our other losses, sinks us, until we find ourselves in a red, sandy grave. In the end, our lives are our deaths. Instinctually C. J. knew this. I have no words.

WE ARE WATCHING
1987–1991

After my father left, we headed to Orange Grove, a neighborhood in Gulfport, Mississippi, a small city a few towns over from DeLisle. Even though Gulfport was within spitting distance of DeLisle, it afforded my mother a certain sense of freedom. She felt smothered in DeLisle, where she knew everyone, and everyone knew her; worse, they were witness to my father's faithlessness. She thought the women of the community gloried in her misfortune, delighted in the way the dissolution of her family became grist for gossip, and judged her for having four children with a fickle man. Gulfport offered anonymity: especially in the many newer subdivisions in the north of the city that were developed in the spare space between new strip malls and grocery stores, neighbors were transient strangers. I was ten, Joshua was seven, Nerissa was five, and Charine was three when we packed our things, boxes of kitchen utensils, our clothes, a few books, and toys, and moved from the home of our extended family into the new house we would live in with our mother, without our father.

Gulfport was not the wilderness we'd been born to in DeLisle. The suburb was off the main highway running north and south through Gulfport. A big wooden sign at the corner of the neighborhood read BEL-AIR. To the west, and closer to the highway, was one of only two undeveloped areas in that section of the city. It was wooded and bordered by baseball fields, cut with a creek, and there were rough trails through it where families sometimes walked on weekends. My mother never allowed us to walk to that park alone for fear that some deranged person would kidnap us. The other undeveloped tract in the area was directly behind our house, which was on the northern edge of the subdivision. It was a rough rectangle, probably a square mile in size, and bordered on all sides by subdivisions filled with small two- and three-bedroom ranch-style houses built in the seventies, all variations on the same three prototypes.

Our house was chocolate-brown brick. There was an anemic tree in the front yard, and a tall deciduous tree in the back that fluttered purple and gray in the light of the city night sky. The backyard was small and surrounded by a metal chain-link fence, like most of the rest in the neighborhood. The houses were so close together we found shade on hot days by sitting in the grassy spots between them.

Moving into the new house that day felt alien and strange. I would be switching schools, and the community of extended family that I knew in DeLisle felt distant in Gulfport. For the first time, we would be a nuclear family, and we would be a nuclear family without a father. The world seemed new and dangerous; I was an animal seeking shelter away from its burrow.

★ ★ ★

BOTH MY PARENTS had been raised without fathers in their homes, and neither of them wanted that for their children. But as children and as adults, a two-parent family eluded them. This tradition of men leaving their families here seems systemic, fostered by endemic poverty. Sometimes color seems an accidental factor, but then it doesn't, especially when one thinks of the forced fracturing of families that the earliest African Americans endured under the yoke of slavery. Like for many of the young Black men in my community across generations, the role of being a father and a husband was difficult for my father to assume. He saw a world of possibility outside the confines of the family, and he could not resist the romance of that. But like many of the young Black women in her generation, my mother understood that she had to forget the meaning of possibility, the tender heat of romance, the lure of the vistas of the world. My mother understood that her vistas were the walls of her home, her children's bony backs, their open mouths. Like the women in my family before her, my mother knew the family was her burden to bear. She could not leave. So she did what her mother did before her, what her sisters did, what her aunts did: she worked and set about the business of raising her children. She did not know it then, but she would be the sole financial provider for us until we reached adulthood.

My mother didn't have many options regarding work: she had a high school diploma, but she had to find jobs that would allow her to be home with her children in the afternoon to ensure we did our homework, took baths, went to bed on time, and got back out the door for school in the morning. If she could have done shift work at one of the vanishing factories, she'd have had access to jobs that paid better, but she couldn't. She had family who would help, but she felt the responsibility of her and my father's choice to have four children keenly; she wouldn't foist the burden of raising us on her extended family, and she wouldn't depend on institutional child care even if she could afford it. She was our mother. So she found jobs that would allow her to raise us. Just before my father left, she worked as a laundress at a hotel in Diamondhead. She carpooled with her cousins to work because she didn't own a car; my father had taken his car and his motorcycle. Before we moved to Gulfport, my mother saved and bought a blue Caprice from the seventies, so old the paint was matte and closing the doors took both hands. This is how she commuted to work at her next job, which was as a housekeeper for a rich White family who lived in an antebellum house on the beach in Pass Christian.

When I was older, she would tell me stories about how she raised her brothers and sisters. She would tell me her father left her family, too, and that she and my father had promised each other when I was born that they would raise their children with both parents. My grandmother worked hard to support her seven children, so it was my mother, the eldest of seven, who rose early in the morning, woke her siblings before school, and made sure they were dressed. She wrangled her sisters' hair into precise pigtails, and when they grew older, she disciplined her brothers and sisters like a mother.

When my parents were together, I thought they were both disciplinarians. My father disciplined my brother, while my mother disciplined all of us. When we moved to Gulfport, I realized that my mother had actually been the disciplinarian all along. Before he left, my father posed us in silly pictures while we held his kung fu weapons and wore bandanas with cryptic kanji characters tied around our skulls. He was the one for riding his bike to the elementary school, parking it out front, and wowing our classmates when we climbed on the back to ride home. My mother cooked the meals, cleaned the house, set us to small chores like emptying the litter box when we had a cat, making our beds, cleaning our rooms, and vacuuming. My father brought in the income, and my mother worked low-paying jobs and kept the household together.

When we moved to Gulfport that summer, my mother taught me that I had a new responsibility in the family: I was the eldest daughter of an eldest daughter, and I had to do as she had done and help keep the household together. Mama bought home a spool of green plastic cording. She dug a hole at the opposite end of the backyard from the tree and slid a wooden cross into the ground. She unspooled the cord and tied it tightly around one side of the cross, and then stretched the cord across the yard and knotted it where a low branch met the trunk of the lone tree. Then she tied another cord to another low branch, and stretched it across the yard to the other side of the cross. She had hung two clotheslines. She unloaded a fresh basket of clothes from the washing machine, walked through the kitchen, and said, "Mimi, come here."

"Yes ma'am."

Joshua and Nerissa and Charine were watching TV. Nerissa followed us out into the yard, while Charine sat in Joshua's lap on the floor in front of the couch.

"Hang up these clothes," she said. She pulled a wet shirt, wrinkled and heavy, from the hamper, and then a clothespin from a bag she'd pinned to the line. She then took a pin from the bag, looped the shirt over the line by its bottom hem, and clipped it to the line.

"This is how you hang shirts. Upside down."

I nodded.

"Pants by the waist."

She handed me a shirt.

"Yes ma'am," I said.

I knew how to do some of it from watching her for years at my grandmother's, where she and her sister washed clothes and sheets for thirteen people and hung them out to dry on lines that stretched the length of the yard. I began hanging on the opposite line: pants crooked, towels like big triangles. Hanging the shirts bothered me. I wanted to hang them from their shoulders because our shirts were constantly stretched out at the hem and hung on our bony frames like A-line skirts, but I did not.

This is how things were done in my mother's house.

MY FATHER'S LEAVING affected me. I locked myself in the bathroom sometimes, which was the only room in our new house where I could claim some privacy, and I looked at myself. I could not see my father in my facial features. He figured prominently in my siblings' large, dark, heavily lashed eyes, but my own seemed small. Too light brown in color. Too sparsely fringed. The rest of my body was also a disappointment: my birth scars mottled and angry and red, my frame weakly muscled, pale. My hair was the opposite of my father's: while his was silky and black, mine was dirty brown and prone to matting. This disappointed me the most. It seemed I had been able to keep nothing of my father. His leaving felt like a repudiation of the child I was and the young woman I was growing into. I looked at myself and saw a walking embodiment of everything the world around me seemed to despise: an unattractive, poor, Black woman. Undervalued by her family, a perpetual workhorse. Undervalued by society regarding her labor and her beauty. This seed buried itself in my stomach and bore fruit. I hated myself. That seed bloomed in the way I walked, slumped over, eyes on the floor, in the way I didn't even attempt to dress well, in the way I avoided the world, when I could, through reading, and in the way I took up as little space as possible and tried to attract as little notice as I could, because why should I? I was something to be left.

I was too young to realize this, but others saw the self-loathing sprouting in me, and they responded to it. At the end of the summer, my mother enrolled us in the unfamiliar local elementary school. I was in the fifth grade. For the first two weeks of the term before my aptitude test scores were processed, I was in a class with a large boy who singled me out for taunting and abuse. Anytime he found me alone in a corner of the library or near the back of our homeroom, he grabbed me by the joints, pinned me to the floor or to my desk or to a wall, and tried to grab my butt. I yanked away from him and did my best to avoid him, but it did no good. I fought like the rabbit I was: timid until grabbed, and then frantic, kicking and twisting. In three weeks, I moved to a more advanced class. But I did not shed my innate sense of worthlessness. I was friends for around a month with the other three Black girls in the class. Then they began bullying me, and my grades dropped. I was miserable, perpetually afraid, and addled on adrenaline, but secretly I was not surprised by it. I thought I deserved it because others were only seeing what I saw, that I was a miserable nothing, and they were acting accordingly. I was depressed at home when I had no idea what depression was, so much so that my mother became concerned enough to pull me out of the school and enroll me in the middle school in Pass Christian during the winter break.

I was excited and anxious at once. I would know some of the other kids. Most students who graduated from DeLisle Elementary were transferred to Pass Christian middle school. But it would be my second school in half a year, and the other experience had been miserable. What if the bullying continued? I knew without knowing that others would see me as a target, and they did. At Pass Middle, I was bullied by three separate groups of girls. I spent all my spare time in the underequipped library, which seemed to have fewer books than my elementary school. I made only two friends, a Black girl and a Vietnamese girl, and we spent our time eating crackers we'd stolen out of the cafeteria, talking about boys and books. I felt more of a kinship with the Vietnamese girl; she was as much of an outsider as I was. I spent my time with her trying to learn Vietnamese through Vietnamese pop songs she taught me. But I was alone in the locker rooms, in the gym, in most of my classes with all the other groups of bullies, and my grades continued to slide southward.

My mother didn't know what to do. Her understanding of my hatred for myself was muddied, unclear. Instead of seeing it as directed at myself, she read it as a sullen anger, a prepubescent hatred that was aimed at her for leaving my father and breaking up the family. This made her pull me even closer, demand even more of me as a cleaner and caretaker in the household. She thought she could discipline it out of me, this sulky hatred. When I turned twelve, I began watching my siblings alone while my mother was at work. My mother knew I was still smart even though my grades were plummeting, so when the employer she'd worked for as a housekeeper since leaving my father and moving to Gulfport asked about my grades, she was honest. Her employer was a White lawyer who'd attended Harvard and practiced corporate law in New Orleans, and in her early days of working for the family, he'd heard stories about her oldest, who was smart, who'd excelled in public school and been in gifted programs. My mother told him that my grades were bad. That I was being bullied at all the schools I attended. Perhaps her employer had been bullied as a child, because even though he had the build of a linebacker, he was soft-spoken and gentle, which would be easy for others to read as weakness. Whatever his reasons, it was unusual, but he offered to pay my tuition to attend the private Episcopalian school his children attended. My mother, always loath to accept help after being betrayed by my father (when he left, she had no credit because he'd had all the cars and bills in his name, and she was left with four children to feed and a nonexistent financial history; she still hates to accept help today, for fear that after it's given it will be taken back), mulled it over for a bit but then accepted the offer. When she asked me if I wanted to switch schools, I gladly accepted. I think my mother would have worked for the family whether or not the husband offered to pay for my schooling, but in accepting his offer, I'd locked her into this employment situation for at least six more years, the time I would need to graduate from high school, regardless of whether she was happy or wanted to work elsewhere. But she saw no other options; this was the job she would work to provide for her children so she could still have enough time out of work to raise them. She would not be an absent mother.

I wasn't the only one having trouble in school. Joshua was only doing enough work to scrape by in second grade. Nerissa was also having trouble in kindergarten; her teacher sent her to the school counselor, who called my mother in for a conference and told her she thought Nerissa had an attention disorder and should be medicated. My mother refused. Charine was oblivious and swimming through preschool. My mother tried her best to support us academically at home. Homework was always a priority. But all of us felt our father's loss keenly, and this sense of being lost and unbalanced found its way into our schoolwork. Even though she tried her hardest, our mother could not be there in school with us during the day; there were some ways that our mother could not help us. Every day after school, we sat at the table with our books, all of us desperately trying to do better and all aware, in the bewildered way that children are, that we were failing.

★   ★   ★

MY FATHER HAD visited once or twice since we'd moved into the house in Gulfport, and when he did, our mother spoke to him briefly and then confined herself to the kitchen or to her room, her door shut. Often she listened to us talking to him, dancing around him, dizzy with longing. It must have been palpable to her, how we changed when we were around him; he had the luxury of being emotionally engaging and attentive while he was with us, while my mother, ever the disciplinarian, felt that she could not. Perhaps she saw in our worshipful faces some of what she'd felt toward her father when she was a child. Perhaps this was why, unbeknownst to us, she began talking to my father about reconciliation.

On his third or so visit, my father sat in the living room, a tray on his lap. My mother had cooked for him, served him food; usually she ignored him. After we'd eaten, we all sat in the living room, watching television, until my mother told us to take baths. We did, and then she sent us to our rooms. Nerissa, Charine, and I lay in the dark, undulating gently on the waterbed. Nerissa and Charine fell asleep, but I was awake, waiting for the side door to open, to close, for my father to catch his ride, or for my mother to take him wherever he was living at the time. He'd been drifting from job to job since leaving my mother, and at the time he was unemployed. He'd wrecked his motorcycle and his car was broken. But the sound of the door didn't come. I eased off the bed, hoping I wouldn't wake my sisters, and crawled across the floor to the door of our room. I eased it open. All the lights were off in the house except my mother's, and her door was closed. I crawled out into the hallway to my brother's room.

"Josh?"

"Huh?"

"You up?"

Stupid question. I crawled into the room, stopped beside the bottom bunk bed.

"Daddy ain't left yet."

"I know," he said.

I didn't know what else to say. We sat in the dark for a while, listening to the other rooms, hearing nothing, talking once in a while: *Do you hear that? Do you think?* We wondered in silence if our father had returned. I sat on Joshua's floor and lay my head on his bed. Josh's breathing grew deeper, until I could tell he was asleep. When he snored, I crawled back to our room, afraid to walk, afraid for my mother to find I was out of bed when I shouldn't be. I climbed into bed with my sisters, pushing Charine over to sleep next to Nerissa, but it was a long time before I fell asleep, my heart beating wildly in my chest with hope and fear.

This is how my father came back.

AFTER MY FATHER moved his clothing and his kung fu knick-knacks in with us, his dream, he told my mother, was to open a kung fu school. Perhaps having my father vocalize his dreams made her realize how strongly my father yearned for them. My mother acquiesced: *You can do it,* she said. He would take his children on as his first students, recruit others, find a space. *Okay,* my mother said. What my mother left unsaid: *I'll keep working, supporting us all, while you try to live your dream.* Her sacrifice remained unacknowledged. *One day,* my father said, *the school will support the family.* I think a part of my mother wanted to believe that this was the truth, so she agreed.

First, my father arranged to teach classes in an after-school program in Biloxi, and then he arranged to teach a class at a dance studio in Pass Christian, and another in Gulfport. He recruited students. The Biloxi program never had more than two, so he cancelled those classes and concentrated on the others, which had more, around ten in Pass Christian and fifteen in Gulfport. He carted us around with him to classes four out of five nights of the week, classes that lasted three hours at a time. We were decent students; he'd taught us forms and one-step sparring since we'd lived in my grandmother's house in DeLisle. We learned the Eight Elbow form out on the patchy, sandy front yard. In our classes in Gulfport and Pass Christian, my father made us do endless sets of sit-ups, push-ups on our knuckles, forms, and sparring. While this was a great start for his business, there still wasn't enough money coming in from students to cover expenses. Once he paid to rent the spaces, there was barely enough money to put gas in the car. This became apparent to me one night after our kung fu class. We were all in the car, including my cousin Aldon, leaving Pass Christian and returning to Gulfport. I noticed the car was gradually slowing.

"We ran out of gas," my father said. I thought he was playing a joke on us. I started laughing.

"No, really," he said.

"We're running out of gas?" Josh asked. Aldon sat up straighter beside him and leaned forward. The car rolled to a stop. The road was dark.

"We have to push," my father said. "Everybody but Nerissa and Charine out of the car." This meant me, Josh, and Aldon. I was twelve, and they were both nine. We were all sore from our workout, still in our uniforms.

"Out," my father said.

We got out.

"Come on, it'll be fun," he said, his teeth white in the dark. There were streetlights every quarter mile or so, but no traffic on this lonely country road, and my father didn't want to leave us alone with the car. "There's a gas station up at the corner. We need to make it to the pay phone." We nodded. "Now, I'm going to steer and push from the front, while y'all three get in the back. Grab the bumper. . . . Yeah, that's it." My father walked around to the front of the car, leaned into the driver's-side door, and grunted, straining.

"Now push!" he said.

We leaned against the car. It rocked but did not move.

"Come on. You have to push harder!"

We dug the toes of our tennis shoes into the rutted asphalt and pushed with our legs, our backs, our arms. We grunted like our father, straining, and the car rolled forward so slowly I could hardly believe it budged.

"Keep going!" Daddy said. "It's right up the road."

It wasn't right up the road. It was at least a half mile up the road, but I didn't know that. Every time I felt like I couldn't push any longer, like my arms had burned to ash and my legs would crumple under me, I wanted to ask my father, *Are we almost there? How close are we?* But I wouldn't. I didn't have the energy to, and he wouldn't have heard me anyhow. Instead I stared at the faint gleam of the car in the darkness and listened to Joshua and Aldon, on both sides of me, breathing in quick little huffs. I imagined a car coming up behind us, slowing to pass us, and then rolling down a window, offering us a ride to a gas station, gas from a spare gas can they kept in the back of their truck, anything so I could stop straining with everything in me, but no cars came. No kind strangers appeared. The air was warm as tepid bathwater, and as close, and the night bugs and the wind were the only things singing and moving in the patches of woods and yards around us. The final stretch of road before the store was up a hill, a steep hill. My father sounded like something in him tore when we crested the hill and rolled into the driveway of the closed gas station, and I felt quivery and soft: useless. The car came to a stop in the parking lot, which had been paved so long ago that it had been ground to gravel. My dad fished out a quarter from his gym bag in the car and dialed my mother from the pay phone on the sidewalk that fronted the shuttered corner store. Joshua and Aldon and I climbed into the car, so tired we didn't speak. Nerissa and Charine slept in the front seat. My father joined us. He too was quiet until my mother arrived with a can full of gas.

"When we get home, y'all need to take a bath and get in bed," she said as she handed my father the gas can. It was late. Her mouth was tight. She climbed back into her car, which she had left running, and waited for us.

I IMAGINE MY mother nursing her resentment that her hard work, her cleaning of toilet bowls and mopping of four-thousand-square-foot houses, was allowing my father to pursue his dream. I imagine that the reality of pursuing his dream took my father aback; that in his head, he saw himself with eager, malleable students like a wise martial arts master in the kung fu films we sometimes watched as a family on Sundays. For those masters, money was never a concern, and they seemed to be childless. I imagine both my parents began to resent their roles in the family. My mother's coping mechanism for this was to become even more silent, even more strict and remote; one of my father's was to watch movies, which was an escape he could share with us.

MY FATHER LED us through the woods behind our house into a cluster of backyards and on through the neighborhood to a strip mall along Dedeaux Road in Gulfport. At the video store, my father would pick out three movies he wanted to see, and then he allowed me and Joshua to pick the other.

Joshua and I lived in the horror section. We stood side by side, studying the pictures on the movie cases, which were always badly drawn and mildly threatening. I read the synopses seriously, ravenously, which was the way I read books. After we'd rented all the store's mainstream horror movies, we began renting the less well-known: movies with leprechauns and ghoulies and blobs and strange sewer-dwelling animals. My mother purchased a popcorn machine, and most weekends found us on the carpeted floor with a big bowl of popcorn between us. It was the cheapest way for my parents to entertain four children. We loved it. For those hour-and-a-half increments, the fantasy of a two-parent family, what we'd longed for in my father's absence, lived for us in perfect snatches. Ignorant of my father's and mother's dissatisfaction, we were butter-faced and giggling and happy.

ONE NIGHT IN the winter of 1990, my mother received a phone call. It was from a woman she knew from DeLisle, who worked at the local police department in Gulfport.

"Do you know where your car is?"

When the woman told my mother the address, my mother knew where my father was. He was with his teenage love. He had parked my mother's car around the corner from his girl's house. I assume he'd told my mother he wasn't seeing her anymore, that he was committed to their relationship and to raising a family together while she worked and he tried to establish his martial arts school. She wouldn't have taken him back without those words. I can imagine the dread she felt when she heard that woman's voice on the phone, the way it washed to pain across her chest before it sank to her stomach. She would have sat for a moment when she got off the phone, staring at the floor, looking at a wall, hearing us through the perfect, awful silence in her head fussing or playing or watching TV in the background. My mother would have steeled herself, but this steel would have been worked thin, thin as aluminum over her love. And underneath it all would have been fatigue. Her joints would have hurt, the marbles of her knuckles already releasing a steady, slim stream of pain that would, five years later, be diagnosed as arthritis. This was what it meant to clean. This was what it meant to work. This was what it meant to forget whatever she had dreamed the night before and to stand up every day because there were things that needed to be done and she was the only person who could do them.

She told me to watch my siblings, and she walked out of the door to get her car. She'd purchased a second car by then, a small blue Toyota Corolla, a stick shift that was new enough to shine a slick blue. She drove to the girl's house, looked past the girl as she sat in my father's lap, and told my father to get in the Caprice and drive it home, and once he did that, she said, he could get the fuck out.

My father has always worn his dreams on the outside, so even as a preteen I knew what they were. I'd known for years he'd wanted to have his own school. He had other dreams that I recognized but still can't articulate, even as I've gotten older. His ill-advised motorcycle purchase; his leather suits, studded and fringed, that he wore in ninety-degree weather; the Prince he listened to on his Walkman while he rode: there was something at the heart of my father that felt too big for the life he'd been born into. He was forever in love with the promise of the horizon: the girls he cheated with, fell in love with, one after another, all corporeal telescopes to another reality.

My mother had buried her dreams on that long ride from California to Mississippi. She'd secreted them next to my brother in the womb, convinced as she was, with a sinking dread, that they were futile. She'd tried to escape the role she'd been born to, of women working, of absent fathers, of little education and no opportunity. She'd tried to escape the history of her heritage, just as my father had. Going to California to join my father had been her great bid for freedom. When she returned, she thought it had failed. She'd returned to the rural poverty, the persistent sacrifice that the circumstance of being poor and Black and a woman in the South demanded. But the suggestion of that dream lived on in her conception of my father. It's part of why she loved him so long and so consistently, and it is part of the reason it hurt her so to meet him at the door with his leather jackets, black sweatpants, and black fringed T-shirts shoved in garbage bags and to tell him: *Go*.

And just like that, my father left.

WITH MY FATHER gone, I picked up my mantle of responsibility. Perhaps if we'd still been in DeLisle, maintaining our family would have been a little easier, but in Gulfport, my mother couldn't bear the burden of the entire family by herself. I was learning that. My mother gave me a house key. It was one item in a growing list of responsibilities. In addition to hanging clothes, gathering them, folding them, putting them away, vacuuming, dusting, cleaning the bathrooms, babysitting my brother and sisters during the day during the summer while my mother was at work, the key meant that during the school year I should let us in the house if we got home from school before my mother made it home from work. But even as a young teen, I was absentminded, forgetful. In the summer, I often left my key inside and turned the lock on the knob and pulled the door shut behind us, locking us out of the house. After our father left, there was no one to open the door if our mother wasn't home. During the school year, I didn't realize I'd left the key at school until I stood before the door with my brothers and sisters.

I patted my short pockets, Josh at my elbow, Charine on my hip.

"I forgot the key."

"What?" Joshua said.

I fumbled around Charine's leg, tried to make her slide down my hip to stand, but she wouldn't.

"I'm so stupid!" I said.

I looked at Josh. He was only a few inches shorter than me, even though he was just nine. He rolled his eyes.

"I have to pee," Nerissa said.

"Me too. I have to pee too," said Charine.

"We going to have to go in the woods."

"I don't want to go in the woods," Nerissa said.

"Me neither," Charine said.

Joshua followed us as I grabbed Nerissa by the hand. I led them around the yard and into the woods we'd walked through with our father to get to the video store; we weren't allowed to walk all the way to Dedeaux Road without him. Fifteen feet into the woods, next to a trail on the right, was a dense cluster of bushes. Further behind the cluster of bushes was a full-size mattress that someone had dumped, probably the previous tenants who'd lived in our house. This, I thought, would have to do.

"Come on," I said. I led them behind the screen of bushes. Charine began to cry. She was convinced that when she pulled down her pants something would bite her. A snake, she said. Or ants.

"Ain't no snakes," I said, although it was summer and hot, and the underbrush could be teeming with them, reptiles cooling themselves in the hottest part of the day.

She resisted.

"You want to pee on yourself?" I threatened. Sobbing, she squatted. I felt guilty for bullying her. "That wasn't that bad," I said. Charine nodded and wiped the snot from her nose with her hand. Josh, who'd watched the path for us, ran past us to the mattress.

"I'm going to do a flip," he said. He sprinted and leapt on the mattress. I expected to see him spring high into the air, soar into a flip. He bounced about a foot or so. The ground had no spring, and the mattress was a sorry trampoline. Still, he did the front flip and landed on his back. When he stood, he smiled dizzily, swaying, and began to bounce again. Nerissa skipped to join him, and Charine let my hand go and ran for the mattress as well, snakes and ants forgotten.

Even though I felt the weight of responsibility with my father gone, as my mother had felt it when hers left (except in even larger measure), I was still a kid. We were still kids, in love with the mystery and beauty of the woods, deriving a certain pleasure out of our scrappy self-imposed exile from the house. We ran wild in the hours between our dismissal from school and my mother's return from work.

ONE DAY, WHILE I was sitting with Charine and Nerissa and weaving flowers into rings and necklaces, Josh appeared and sat with us. He'd been off exploring.

"I found something," he said.

"What is it?"

"A secret room," Josh said. "I'ma show you."

We followed him further into the woods, along the trail

that curved to the right, the trail that would take us through the subdivision and to a corner store on Dedeaux Road if we followed it. We walked in single file because it was so narrow. Underbrush and weeds grew thickly off the dirt path, scratched our calves, our shins. I picked Charine up and carried her. She was four. Joshua led and Nerissa trotted on his heels, proud to be keeping up with him, even at six. Then he led us off the trail, and I hoisted Charine around to my back and bent, all of us burrowing our way through thorny, leaf-drenched bushes, stumbling through blackberry brambles as the pines shivered above our heads. Suddenly the woods opened up into a small clearing. The ground was soft and spongy below our feet, padded with layers of pine straw.

"Watch," Josh said, and knelt. He felt in the straw along what looked like a shallow ditch, then pushed the earth. There was a scraping sound. The straw moved, and there was a black hole where the ditch had been. "Look," he said.

We clustered behind him. I grabbed Nerissa's hand and leaned over Josh's narrow back before I understood what I was seeing. Someone had dug into the earth, made a cellar, and then covered it over with two-by-fours before strewing pine straw to camouflage it.

"Who made this?" I asked.

"I don't know," Joshua said. He had friends in the neighborhood, too, Black boys and one White boy, all who, like my girlfriend, lived there with their single mothers. *Maybe they made it,* I thought, but it seemed too large an undertaking for skinny little kids with knees like doorknobs, shirtless boys whose ribs you could count when they rode their bikes through the streets. *So much digging,* I thought. *And planning.*

"Let's go," I said. I pulled Nerissa's arm.

"You don't want to go down in it?" Joshua asked. I could tell by the way he said it that he hadn't gone down in it yet, and that he thought we might explore it together.

"No," I said. "Let's go."

I yanked Nerissa to walk.

"Hold on," I told Charine, and she tightened her legs around my waist, locking them at the heels. I pushed branches out of the way, began shouldering through the underbrush back to the trail. Josh stood behind us, still at the mouth of that hole.

"Come on!" I said.

He hesitated, then followed. When we reached the trail, I began trotting, Charine bouncing up and down on my back, laughing.

"Run," I said.

We ran, stumbling on roots, plants whipping us like fishing line at the ankle. When we reached the end of the trail, we ran past the mattress, leapt over the ditch that bordered the woods and our yard, then let ourselves into the fence and the backyard, where we stopped, breathing hard. I turned on the hose and made everyone drink, and I kept us close to the yard for the rest of the day. Josh did a few desultory flips on the mattress, but he was the only one who reentered the woods before coming back out again.

That night, after my mother had fussed at me for forgetting my key again, after we'd all been bathed and ordered to bed, I lay awake in the dark, staring at the ceiling, trying to see the dresser, our stuffed animals, my lonely fish in its small, plastic rectangular tank the size of a saucer. I wanted them to glow brightly, to pacify me and let me know I was not alone, but they stood silently in the darkness, beyond my view. I was tempted to shake Nerissa awake so she'd open her eyes because I knew they would be white in the dark and she would at least grunt at me, but I did not. Along with the responsibilities I'd resumed when my father left again, his departure renewed my sense of abandonment, worthlessness. While I lay next to my sleeping sisters, questioning my father's love, I equated the cellar out in the woods with my deserved misery. Instead of waking Nerissa, I pictured the open mouth of that cellar off in the darkness, in the future, gaping as a grave.

THE NEXT DAY, I didn't ask my friend Kelly about the cellar, or my friend Tamika, or my friend Cynthia. Instead, I stood barefoot in the empty lot next to our house, still thinking about it, while half listening to Kelly talk.

"Girl, have you heard that new song by that White rapper?"

I looked confused.

"He is so fine," she said. I was thirteen by then, all slim lines and teeth and unruly hair that my mother had first given up on combing, and then attempted to tame with a relaxer. When Kelly said this, she smiled and her entire body shook, the woman parts of her moving like water. Kelly was fourteen. She rolled her eyes.

"Wait till you see him."

When I saw him on television, the White rapper was all hard lines and sequins. There were other boys I saw in the neighborhood who I thought were more attractive, boys with prominent cheekbones and black hair and dark, almost black eyes. Boys who looked like my father when he was younger. But I had no boyfriends. I thought I was too skinny and ugly to get a boyfriend: I would never approach and speak to a boy I didn't know, and most times they wouldn't approach me either. And if they did, I didn't feel flattered. I felt embarrassed. But Kelly had boyfriends, and so did Crissy, one of my friends from the middle school in Pass Christian. We still talked on the phone sometimes, and she told me stories.

"I almost had sex," she said.

"Huh?"

"I did."

"Really?"

"My boyfriend came over and my mama wasn't home. We was in the room and we was kissing and stuff. He tried to put it in, but it wouldn't go."

"Oh," I said, amazed at her brazenness.

"I guess that meant God didn't think it was the right time," she said.

We were thirteen, but even so I was surprised by her mention of God. My ideas about God at the time were that He'd have nothing whatsoever to do with sanctioning an unwed woman, a teenager, having sex, so I didn't understand Crissy's logic.

"I guess not," I said.

We weren't allowed to let kids into our house when our mother was at work for the day, and mostly I didn't want to. We met our friends on the street or in the woods, and in Gulfport, all of my friends were girls. Even though my girlfriends were dating, I didn't want to. I was still reading books and playing with dolls in secret. I let a boy into my mother's house once when she was at work, but I did not let him in because I thought he was attractive, or because I wanted something to happen between us; I let him and his friend in because I thought they were Joshua's friends. It was a disaster. It was a few weeks after we'd found the cellar, and two boys we knew from the neighborhood came by. Phillip was actually Joshua's friend, skinnier than my brother and maybe a few inches taller, and he liked to wear his hair in a lopsided Gumby cut. His friend was a boy named Thomas, who was around my age, twelve, and we didn't know him well. He was taller than Phillip, by at least a foot, and thick. He had a wide, flat nose, and his shoulders seemed lopsided, set at an angle, like whatever aligned him was askew.

"Can we come in?" Thomas asked.

Joshua and Charine and Nerissa were in the living room, watching *You Can't Do That on Television*, and I stood at the side door that opened to the carport. The day was bright and hot beyond them, the bugs loudly lamenting the heat. The house was cool, even though my mother kept the thermostat at eighty to save money on her electricity bill during the summertime. We were threatened with whipping if we changed the setting. We never did.

"I guess," I said.

The two boys followed me into the living room. Phillip sat on the sofa next to Josh, and they began talking. I sat on the long sofa. Nerissa and Charine looked up from their playing for a moment, dolls in mid-meal on the floor, and then went back to it.

"Can I sit next to you?" Thomas asked.

"I guess," I said.

Thomas sat next to me on the sofa.

"What y'all been doing today?"

"Nothing," I said. "Watching TV."

"It's hot out there."

"Yeah."

Thomas scooted closer. His leg touched mine. I scooted over, further into the crack of the sofa.

"Where y'all mama?"

"Work," I said.

Thomas edged closer so his leg was touching mine again, and I tried to scoot over, but I was jammed into the arm of the sofa. I couldn't understand why he wasn't talking to Josh and Phillip.

"Why you keep scooting over?" Thomas asked.

I shrugged, turning a shoulder to him and leaned away from his face. Josh and Phillip, still talking and laughing, walked out the side door. It closed behind them.

"I like you," Thomas said.

I was mute. He pressed against me, sandwiching me between him and the cushions. I half stood, and he grabbed my arm and yanked me back down to the sofa.

"You don't like me?" he said.

I shook my head. His hand slid up my arm, to my shoulder, my neck. I jerked away from him, and he moved with me. I was helpless.

"Stop," I said. It was a squeak.

"What? I'm not doing anything."

"Stop touching me," I said. *I deserve this,* I thought.

"Come on, girl," he said, leaning into me again, leading with his mouth. He grabbed my arm hard. *This is my fault,* I thought. Charine and Nerissa were quiet.

"Stop it!" I couldn't breathe. He was too big. *Just sit there, and if you take it long enough, it'll be over,* I thought.

Charine jumped up from her squat on the floor and ran toward the sofa. She leapt into Thomas's lap feet first and began jumping on him, stomping his crotch.

"Leave my sister alone! Leave my sister alone!" she yelled.

"Get off me," he said, trying to push her away, sliding over enough that I was able to get up and away from him. I stood.

"Leave her alone!" Charine said, kicking. Nerissa was crying. I scooped Charine up under her armpits and swung her to my waist. She had given me my voice back.

"Get out!" I said.

"What?"

"Get out!" I said. "Or I'm going to call my mama!"

He jumped up from the sofa. I ran to the side door, Charine still on my hip, and swung the door open wide, letting in the heat of the day.

"Out!"

He walked past and out into the heat, looking down at us.

"Fuck you," he said.

"Fuck you!" I said, slamming the door, locking the deadbolt. I was surprised I could be so angry.

Thomas hit the door, hard.

"You stupid bitch!" he said.

"I'm not a bitch!" I said. But even as I said it, I was ashamed for not fighting back earlier on the sofa. *I had to be saved by a three-year-old,* I thought.

"Fucking slut!" He hit the door again.

I backed away from it, Charine clinging to me. We stared at the shuddering door: Charine was alert, ready to go at him again. *I'm pathetic,* I thought. There was a knocking at the back door, and then Josh opened it and walked inside. I locked that one, too.

"What you locked the side door for?" Josh asked. Thomas banged again. I could hear Phillip laughing on the carport.

"Him," I said, pointing at the side door.

"Bitch!" Thomas hit it again. There was quiet on the other side. I put Charine down, walked to the front window, knelt, and peered through the blinds as the two boys skipped out in the sun and slowed to a walk in the middle of the street. I watched them until they disappeared around the corner of the house.

It didn't matter if my mother was home or not. Thomas caught me out when I was hanging clothes by myself or sweeping the carport. He wouldn't come into the yard, but he would roam the edges of the fence, the woods at the back of the house, scream, *I know you hear me talking to you. You hear me talking to you.* And then: *I see you.* When he said this, I thought he meant that he saw all the misery in me, saw that I deserved to be treated this way by a boy, any boy, all boys, everyone, and I believed him.

MY MOTHER WITHDREW after my father left. When she was home, she was cleaning. Or she was in the kitchen, cooking. There were no more movie marathons. We had food stamps then, books of them that I was always embarrassed to spend at the Colonial Bread store, but my mother had no compunctions about using them to keep the refrigerator stocked. Unlike my father, my mother wasn't comfortable with physical shows of affection. She didn't hug us or kiss us or touch us when she talked to us, like he did. Sometimes I think that my mother felt that if she relaxed even a tiny bit, the world she'd so laboriously built to sustain us would fall apart. So since she couldn't overtly express her love for us, which was as large and fierce and elemental as the forest fires that sometimes swept through the woods behind our house, she showed us she loved us the only way she knew how beyond providing a home for us, cleaning, taking care of us, providing discipline: through food. She cooked huge pots of gumbo, beef and vegetable soup, pork chops, mashed potatoes, roasts, red beans and rice, cornbread, and desserts—pecan candy, blueberry muffins, German chocolate cakes, and yellow sheet cakes that she decorated with elaborate flowers and vines made of frosting.

When she wasn't cooking, she was in her room watching television. She had one friend in the neighborhood, a woman who'd married my mother's distant cousin. They lived across the street. My mother's cousin was struggling with drug addiction, so my mother bought his wife and family food sometimes, allowed her children to come inside our house when they came over to play. My mother had one close friend who was also her cousin, who'd moved away to Atlanta. Other than that, she was alone. Even as she nurtured a general suspicion of men, she saw the cunning, messy cruelty of women, too; the various women my father had affairs with, some of whom had been her friends, some of whom had known her

since they'd been children, had gloried in my mother's dis-
grace, had called her and told her: *He doesn't love you—he
loves me.* She didn't trust women or men. Her children were
her only company, but we were a boisterous, gregarious tribe
she loved wholeheartedly yet had little patience for, since she
had been raising children her entire life. All the choices and
all the circumstance of her existence heated to a rolling boil
that summer of 1990, boiled and bubbled over and burned
her. It was too much for one person to bear. She stumbled.

When one of us did something wrong, like leaving our
clothes on the bathroom floor one too many times after bathing, or getting into arguments with each other and fighting,
she whipped all of us. Sometimes she used the short shaft of
a wooden toy broom. When Joshua found it one day while she
was at work, he snuck out into the woods and threw it away.
She bought another one. After months of touching us only
when she physically disciplined us, she switched to psycho-
logical tactics. One day she threatened to give us up for
adoption, and when she heard me crying in our room late at
night, she called me to her doorway and asked me why.

"Because you said you want to give us up," I said.

"Maybe if y'all weren't so bad," she said, "I wouldn't have
to threaten y'all."

And still we felt our behavior would never be good enough.
I was failing her. Driven by her sense of isolation or loneliness or a desire to reveal something about her sense of discipline to me or to warn me against what she might have seen
of her legacy coming to life in me, she parked her car in the
carport after a trip to the store one day and told me brother
and sisters to go inside, and then said to me: "Wait—stay

here." And then she did something that must have been incredibly hard for her since it was so opposite to her nature; she talked to me. She told me stories. "Mimi," she said, "your father . . ." And then she opened herself up in ways she wouldn't do for many years. She told me some things I understood at the time, and other things I wouldn't understand until I was her age, and other things I still don't understand, about how she grew up as the caretaker for her brothers and sisters, about her relationship with her mother, about how she loved her father and her husband and lost them both, again and again. At thirteen, I glimpsed something of what my mother had suffered. For an afternoon, I knew some of my mother's burdens, some of which mirrored my own. For a moment, I felt keenly what it meant to be my mother's daughter. For a little while, I was wiser than I had the maturity to be, and I did what I could. I listened.

AND MY MOTHER listened too, when she could, to our furtive whisperings. We missed DeLisle, we said. We missed running barefoot along the dirt roads and eating blackberries, hot with juice and sugar and sun, and floating in the current of the river. We didn't like walking in a little tight group down to Bel-Air Elementary in the summer to eat free lunch in the cafeteria, feeling awkward and poor. So she asked us: "Do y'all want to move back to DeLisle?" And we said yes.

My mother, frugal by necessity, had saved enough money to buy half an acre of land from her father's sister. In the summer of 1990, she set out to clear it, armed with machetes and chainsaws along with her brothers. Sometimes she brought us along on her days off that summer before we moved, and sometimes she didn't. On one of the days when she didn't, Joshua and I left Nerissa and Charine in the house and walked back into the woods. If my mother knew, she'd be angry I left my two youngest siblings alone, but I wanted to see that cellar again. I needed to see if it still gaped in that small clearing. I didn't fully understand that it had taken on a symbolic importance for me, a physical representation of all the hatred and loathing and sorrow I carried inside, the dark embodiment of all the times in Gulfport when I had been terrorized or sexually threatened. I didn't understand that it had become an omen for me. When Joshua and I got there, we found the plywood that had covered the top of the cellar gone, so what remained was a large, open ditch lined with pine straw, perfectly square and dark. Somehow it was even more awful to see the dim recesses of that man-made hole, and my response was visceral. I felt as if I were down in it, as if my world had shrunk to its confines: the pine straw pricking my legs and arms, the walls a cavern around me, tall as a line of trees, the sky itself obscured. I couldn't escape it. Its specter would follow me my entire life. Joshua and I stared into its maw without talking, and then left. I wonder if he felt something as well, standing there on the crumbling edge of that awful hole, of the awful future we would bear.

The house was messy. I was grateful that at least Nerissa and Charine hadn't broken anything. I set Nerissa and Charine to small tasks, picking up their toys in the living room, while I washed dishes. Joshua was outside in the backyard. I walked to the window with wet and soapy hands to talk to him.

"Josh," I said, "you need to come inside and take out the trash."

"All right," he said.

I washed a sinkful of cups and moved on to bowls. He still wasn't inside. I walked to the window again.

"Josh!" I said. I was frustrated: I felt the weight of being a child with adult responsibilities. I was inadequate. I was failing.

My brother stood out in the yard, peering into the dark of the house. He wasn't looking up at me, and I realized that he and I were the same height now. His hair was a sandy brown in the sun he squinted against, and his black T-shirt was fitted on his frame, pulled so by the way he was gaining weight at eleven. Joshua looked through the screen and it was as if he saw me clearly with my soapy hands, my wrinkled fingers, my jaw grinding with frustration and self-abasement, and he hated me. Both of us on the cusp of adulthood, and this is how my brother and I understood what it meant to be a woman: working, dour, full of worry. What it meant to be a man: resentful, angry, wanting life to be everything but what it was.

RONALD WAYNE LIZANA

BORN: SEPTEMBER 20, 1983
DIED: DECEMBER 16, 2002

HE'S GOING TO be a heartbreaker when he grows up.

Ronald was nine then, and I was fifteen, but it was still evident even then, in his short, even-limbed frame, that he would grow yet more beautiful when he became older. He was light on his feet, seemed to be perpetually on his tiptoes, ready to prank, run, and disappear down the elementary school hallway. He reminded me of Joshua at that age. Ronald too was an only boy in a family of girls; I'd attended elementary school with his oldest sister. Teachers would stop his sister and me at play and ask if we were related. They'd say: *Y'all look alike.* Ronald looked even more like Josh standing next to my cousin Tony, who was also nine, but who was around three shades darker than Ronald.

I was a counselor at All God's Critters day camp. It was sponsored by my high school, Coast Episcopal, and was designed to provide free summer activity for underprivileged kids. As a student, I could volunteer to be a counselor; as underprivileged kids, most of the kids I knew in DeLisle and Pass Christian were eligible to go, but only three of them attended

that summer: Antonio, my cousin Rajea, and Ronald. I wrote
Tony's name in the attendance book.

"And who's this?" I smiled at Ronald. He smiled back
slowly: his teeth white, his skin copper, his eyes large and
brownish black. He had a smattering of freckles across his
nose. *He's going to get all the girls*, I thought.

"Ronald Lizana," he said. I wrote his name in the book.

"You'll be with the other boys," I said. "Come on. I'll take
y'all to your station." I wrote Rajea's name and grabbed her
hand, leading her down the hallway. I looked back to make
sure Ronald and Tony were following. Ronald grinned at
Tony, and Tony started laughing at a private joke.

I'd volunteered as a counselor for the Christian day camp
because I wanted to get out of the house for the two weeks
the camp ran. By this time, Josh was old enough to watch
Nerissa and Charine during the day while I was at camp and
Mama was at work. My brother and sisters hadn't wanted to
go to the camp; they thought it was lame. "All them White
people," they said. "And church." I shrugged. I was on the tail
end of a devout Christian phase, where I spent at least half of
every hour thinking about God, praying, and feeling suf-
fused with divine love. When I'd transferred to the Episcopalian school in sixth grade, I'd found irresistible the idea of
a God who loved me unfailingly, scars and all. Here was a
man who would never leave, I thought. Someone whom I
would never disappoint. Later, I would fall away from the
church when the rigidity of the doctrine and hypocrisy of
some of the most devout Christian students I went to school
with became apparent to me. In the end, I realized sometimes
some people were forsaken.

I was a cheerleader, which meant that instead of teaching
arts and crafts or doing Bible study in the form of singing
Christian folk songs with the other high schoolers and two
seminary students who ran the camp, I taught dance. My
co-counselor and I choreographed and taught the kids rou-
tines to "The Humpty Dance" and "I Wish I Was a Little Bit
Taller," which they were set to perform for the rest of the
camp at the end of the week. On the first day, Ronald was
unimpressed.

"You don't know how to dance," he said.

"Yes I do," I said.

"So you can pop?"

"Yeah."

My co-counselor was teaching the other kids the beginning of the dance and counting: "And one and two and three
and four and five and six and seven and eight . . ."

"Do it."

"I ain't fixing to pop for you."

"I can do it."

"No, you can't."

Tony ambled over.

"Watch," Ronald said. He widened his stance, put his
hands palm down in front of him, and began thrusting his
hips back and forth. I laughed. He *could* pop. Tony joined in.

"We're not putting that in the dance."

"Why not?" Ronald said.

The corners of his mouth twitched. He was a natural flirt.

"You really think the other boys would do it?"

"Yeah," he said.

"You going to do it, Tony?"

"Yeah," he said.

"Okay then." I crossed my arms. "We'll put it in."

RONALD WAS CHARMING, a showoff. As I carried large plastic trays of juice and graham crackers down the narrow school hallway for snack in the afternoon, he'd stop in the dim space outside of the bathroom, pat the air in front of himself, and pop. I'd laugh, the crackers in their cups sliding across the tray, the juice sloshing over the side of the waxed paper cups, rolling in thin streams so that when I finally got to the classroom with the snack, all of the cups bottoms' were soggy.

In dance class, he caught on quickly. He was like C. J., athletic, lean, and short. He was able to pick up movements easily and imbue them with his own character. I thought because Tony and Ronald were such good friends, they'd shrug off my authority, wander off to the back of the classroom to play with the detritus of the school year or disappear into the dim hallways on hourlong bathroom breaks. But they didn't. When I asked them to listen, they did, and they executed all my awkward dance moves, moving gleefully whenever they looked at each other, or whenever they got to the popping eight count.

Towards the end of the two weeks, we made homemade Slip 'n Slides by rolling out long plastic sheets and coating them with dishwashing detergent and water. The sky was a boundless blue, and the air was clear, free of the usual torrents of summer rain. We set both slides side by side on a slight hill in a field.

One of my co-counselors, who was shirtless, pale, and

grinning in the sun, was eager to test the slide. He ran at it, jumped, and flew down the hill on his stomach and off the slide at the end, whizzing across the grass. When he stood, his chest was green and red, and I wondered if it hurt.

"That was awesome," he said.

Ronald and Tony had the same idea.

"Watch this, Mimi!" Tony said. He ran and hurled himself down the slide. The thump sounded as if it hurt, but he grinned into the soapy water, and he flew off the end of the plastic and plowed to a stop in the dirt. Ronald took Tony's success as a challenge. He flung himself at the plastic from a run, and zipped down the slide before landing in the grass. Ronald ran up the hill to the beginning of the slide while Tony zipped down again. I added more water and more soap. The other boys followed suit, whooping and crashing into the lawn. Ronald stopped next to me, blades of grass on his face and in his hair. I brushed them away: his face was hot and clammy under my fingers.

"You should get on it," Ronald said. He spat away a piece of green that had slid to his lip.

"Naw, I don't have a bathing suit."

"Get on in your clothes."

"Then I'll be walking around with wet clothes all day."

"Come on," he said.

"I can't."

I brushed another sliver of grass from his face, and he shivered and smiled. Boys ran by him in pairs. "You're cute," I said. I figured there was no harm in telling Ronald something he already knew.

"One day I'm going to marry you," he said.

"Really?"

"Yep." He nodded, smiling his charming smile.

"You promise?"

"Yeah."

I laughed and brushed away another blade. Ronald ran to the slide and Tony followed and they threw themselves at it, both of them burning darker in the heavy sun. I rolled the sleeves of my T-shirt up so they bunched under my armpits and let my shoulders warm. When I told the boys their session was done, the others ran inside, but Tony and Ronald lagged behind.

"Help me pick up these hoses," I told them. A few clouds scudded across the sky, shadowing them, and when they cleared, Tony and Ronald were carrying empty bottles of dishwashing liquid and dragging hoses, mud and grass smeared across their bellies. The boys saw me watching and stopped to dance in the field, popping while holding the hoses and bottles up. They looked like drunk adults on the edge of a parade, dancing as Mardi Gras floats passed. I laughed. The sun caught them, and they were beautiful.

As RONALD AGED, he got taller: the planes of his face spread and sharpened, his shoulders broadened and his waist slimmed, but when his face dimpled, he was still that nine-year-old boy in the field, shining copper in the sun. Ronald didn't lose his charm and charisma, or his handsomeness, as he grew older. If anything, he was more confident, especially with women. I saw him sometimes around DeLisle or Pass Christian. Sometimes I even saw him around my mother's house when I was home visiting from NYC, since he and Charine were good friends; when he walked through the living room to Charine's room, he always seemed to be smiling, to be leaning forward as he walked, all the angles of his body harmonious like a song. I never imagined that he carried something darker in him, never saw him when his mood was cloudy and he turned furious or depressed. I was too immature to imagine at the time that the darkness that I carried from my prepubescent years, that conviction of worthlessness and self-loathing, could have touched others in my community.

What I did not understand then was that the same pressures were weighing on us all. My entire community suffered from a lack of trust: we didn't trust society to provide the basics of a good education, safety, access to good jobs, fairness in the justice system. And even as we distrusted the society around us, the culture that cornered us and told us were perpetually less, we distrusted each other. We did not trust our fathers to raise us, to provide for us. Because we trusted nothing, we endeavored to protect ourselves, boys becoming misogynistic and violent, girls turning duplicitous, all of us hopeless. Some of us turned sour from the pressure, let it erode our sense of self until we hated what we saw, without and within. And to blunt it all, some of us turned to drugs.

But I did not know this in the spring of 2002, which is why I thought Ronald was happy when I saw him at the park. Nerissa was off sitting in what I later would find out was Demond's car, which was pulled onto the side of the court and parked in the weak seasonal sun, and I was sitting on the bleachers with Hilton watching Ronald play basketball with a girl. I was home, visiting, and it was a relief to sit in the park again, be still under the trees and the great heavy sky.

Ronald was laughing and copping feels on the court. He pulled his sleeves back over his elbows and threw his hands in the air and shoved his crotch into the girl's ass like he was guarding her. She dribbled the ball, bent over, smiled before glancing behind at him. He smiled encouragingly at the stands. This was Ronald's flirting all grown up: knowing and corporeal. Hilton sat beside me, and we laughed at the joke. The girl was coy, noticing what Ronald was doing but not discouraging him. She was a teenager, exuding her budding sexuality with every smile, every jut of her hips as she dribbled, with every giggle. At the opposite end of the court, Charine and C. J. threw the ball to each other, playing a game of twenty-one. After his game with the girl, Ronald climbed the bleachers and sat next to us. Hilton passed him a cigar.

"We still getting married?" I asked.

"Yeah," Ronald said. Hilton snorted. Something about Ronald's face was surprised, pleased. "Hell yeah," he said. The girl wandered off to the cars. After drawing on the cigar, Ronald followed her.

Charine said when they rode around DeLisle later that day, smoking and listening to music and talking shit, I came up in the conversation. Her friends talked about the way I jogged down the street for exercise in sports bra and shorts, hair a rough curly tangle escaping the bun at the back of my head, my right leg kicking out to my side in a circle, my arms hanging low with my hands open. *What are you doing*, one of them had once asked, *running or swimming?* Another would ride behind me on his bike, talking constantly about the neighborhood, about the weather, about the day, about the way the crackheads walked the block, all the while singing lines from the latest songs. Once I told him to get away from me through labored, wet breaths. *That hurts my feelings*, he said. And then: *You still run funny.* Charine and C. J. and their friends talked about me in that car and Ronald stopped them. He passed one of them the blunt.

"Shut up," he said. "That's my wife. Don't talk about my wife."

"Whatever," one of them laughed.

"I'm not playing," he said.

They all laughed and parked in a driveway lined with a column of azalea bushes almost tall as a man, and smoked the afternoon away.

AFTER I SAW Ronald that day at the park, I thought I knew him. I thought that if I were younger and we were in high school together, Ronald was the sort of boy I'd fall in love with: funny, confident, charming, a bit arrogant. But there was much I didn't know about Ronald, about his life and how happy or unhappy he was. He was nineteen. When I saw him, he lived with his mother. They argued, so he moved in with his older sister. After some months, he and his sister argued, he moved out of her house and for a stretch of time in the fall, he was homeless. He squatted in an abandoned house until his older cousin Selina, who was in her early twenties, found out, so she tracked him down and told him, "Kinfolk don't live on the street." Ronald moved in with her.

Ronald snorted cocaine, and he hustled for money. This is

why he fought with his family. They loved him, wanted him to start working and stop using drugs, but he could not. He knew he could not, which is why he told Selina he wanted to go to rehab: he loved his mother and his two sisters, and his estrangement from them pained him. He felt that he couldn't please any of the women in his life, including his girlfriend. The charm and charisma of his youth were as meaningless as a tonsil or appendix in his adult life. He knew how to navigate the world as a child, but as a young Black man, he was unmoored. The hard facts of being a young Black man in the South, the endemic joblessness and poverty, and the ease of self-medicating with drugs disoriented him.

After Ronald moved in with Selina, she visited his mother to assure her that he was safe. She wanted to let his mother know that Ronald was helping out, was almost a father figure to her son, spending his afternoons taking care of him while Selina worked. She wanted to let his mother know he was okay. Ronald's mother expressed her frustration and helplessness in the face of Ronald's addiction. Ronald took this as rejection.

As they lay on their backs on the bed in Selina's bedroom, staring at the ceiling, at a sky he couldn't see, he told Selina: "It's like my mama pushing me in the streets."

"Ain't no way, cuz," Selina said.

"It feel like they do," Ronald said.

"They want you to do better for yourself."

Ronald closed his eyes, tamped something down.

"They want you to get a real job. Do it legally."

★ ★ ★

ONE NIGHT RONALD and Selina took a ride through Pass Christian before parking under the wide, reaching oak trees that screened the city park from Scenic Drive, the highway, and beyond that the beach. My father told me he'd been chased out of that park as a child for being Black, called a nigger by the groundskeeper. The beauty of the massive oaks and the water over the southern horizon belied that history as Selina and Ronald sat in the car and talked about Ronald's demons.

"I was in my sister's car. I parked it right here," Ronald said.

The oaks ignored the beach breeze.

"I had the gun under the seat."

The Spanish moss in the oaks pulled tight as a flag in the wind.

"I pulled it out. I was going to pull the trigger."

The moss wrapped around the trees' limbs and caught.

"And then the phone rang. It was my sister."

"Why?" Selina said.

"I got all these problems."

"Like what?"

"My girlfriend."

"What you mean?"

"She be doing shady shit." He thought she was cheating on him and hiding her infidelities. He channeled all the frustration and darkness of his life into their relationship until their love took on epic proportions.

"They got too many women in the world," Selina said.

"But I love her," Ronald breathed. "I love her to death."

★   ★   ★

THE NIGHT BEFORE Ronald died, he met up with another cousin in Long Beach. They sat out in a car in the parking lot of an apartment complex, smoking and talking.

"I'm going into the military, cuz."

"Oh yeah?"

"Been talking to a recruiter. I'm ready," he said.

His cousin said he seemed optimistic, that the promise represented by the military had given him hope, or so it seemed. He was searching for a way out. But Selina remembers it differently. Her son's birthday was the day before Ronald died, and she'd thrown a party for him, all balloons and party hats and streamers, all baby-boy blue. Ronald called her every other hour, said: "Cuz, I'm coming." Said: "Cuz, I ain't forgot." Said: "Cuz, I'm on my way."

But as the day waned and the party ended, she got another call from one of Ronald's friends, who said: "I saw him at the Shell station. He doesn't look like himself." She looked for him and caught a glimpse outside the station, but something was wrong with his face under the fluorescent lights. When she maneuvered her car back around to return for him, he'd disappeared.

I DON'T KNOW all Ronald's demons. I don't know the specifics of what Ronald ran from, what he felt he was outpacing when he talked about going to rehab or joining the military and if he self-medicated with cocaine so he could feel invincible and believe in a future. I don't know what that debilitating darkness, that Nothing that pursued him, looked like, what shape his depression took. For me, it was a cellar in the woods, a wide, deep living grave. I know what it feels like. I know that sense of despair. I know that when he looked down at his copper hands and in the mirror, at his dark eyes and his freckles and his even mouth, that he thought it would be better if he were dead, because then all of it, every bit of it, would stop. The endless struggle with his girlfriend, the drugs that lit his darkness, the degradations that come from a life of poverty exacerbated by maleness and Blackness and fatherlessness in the South—being stopped and searched by the police, going to a high school where no one really cared if he graduated and went to college, the dashed dreams of being a pilot or a doctor or whatever it was he wanted, realizing that the promises that had been made to him at All God's Creatures day camp were empty and he didn't have a world and a heaven of options—all of these things would cease. And this is what Ronald thought he wanted.

Years later, I searched for and found statistics about mental health and Black people in an effort to understand something about Ronald, about myself, about my community. Racism, poverty, and violence are the primary factors that encourage depression in Black men, and I'd guess that this is true for Black women as well. Seven percent of African American men develop depression during their lifetime, and according to experts, this is probably an underestimate due to lack of screening and treatment services. They will not get care for their mental disorders. The percentage of African Americans, men and women, who do receive care for mental disorders is half that of non-Hispanic Whites. Not treating these mental disorders costs Black men and women dearly, because when mental disorders aren't treated, Black men are more vulnerable to incarceration, homelessness, substance abuse, homicide, and suicide, and all of these, of course, affect not just the Black men who suffer from them but their families and the glue that holds the community together as well. According to "Souls of Black Men: African American Men Discuss Mental Health," Black men's death rates from suicide are twice as high as those for Black women. And when Black males ages fifteen to nineteen years old die by suicide, 72 percent of them use guns to do so.[1]

These statistics punctuate my experience like an exclamation point. I read these and think about what happened to Ronald and feel he intuitively understood what it took me years of suffering grief, battling my own depression, reading, writing to understand. In the end, I understand his desire, the self's desire to silence the self, and thus the world. Ronald looked at his Nothing and saw its long history, saw it in all our families and our communities, all the institutions of the South and the nation driving it. He knew it walked with all of us, and he was tired of walking.

RONALD WAS AT his sister's apartment in a complex in Long Beach. He was there alone. Still, I imagine he went into the bedroom and shut the door when his girlfriend finally answered the phone and they began arguing.

"Why are you acting like this? I love you. Tell me you love me."

---

[1] See www.communityvoices.org/uploads/souls_of_Black_Men_00108_00037.pdf, July 2003.

"No."

"I'm going to kill myself."

"No you're not."

"Yes I am."

"Stop playing."

"I am."

"Whatever, Ronald."

I imagined the apartment had white walls, a dark bed-spread on the double bed in the room, the floor bare besides the carpet. He had to have thought about this, planned it, bor-rowed or traded or bought the gun and bullets for it, been home by himself at a certain time. He had to have felt his Nothing over his shoulder, bearing down on him while spur-ring him into action. He had to have forgotten what it was like to stand outside under the hot Mississippi sun, to burn gold in it, to feel loved and alive and beautiful. He had to have felt like this was the only thing left for him to do. Ronald hung up the phone, shot himself in the head, and died.

CHARINE CALLED ME at work in New York City and told me. I stared at the gray walls of my cubicle, the gray carpet under my feet, the gray buildings through the window, the gray New York sky bounded by skyscrapers, and thought, *Not an-other death.* I hated phones. After I hung up with Charine, I looked at my hands and then walked into my boss's office after knocking timidly on the door frame.

"Come in," she said.

How should I tell her? I thought. *How do I say my friend, a boy I watched dance in the sun, mud-streaked and happy, killed himself?* I think I might have called him my cousin when I told her. I tried not to but began crying, and she frowned with kindness.

"You should go home for the day," she said. I wiped my face with my hands, embarrassed that I was crying in public, walked out, powered down my computer, and left work. I rode home on the deserted subway in the middle of the day, glaring at every person I saw. I walked through crowds on the street and thought I had never been in so crowded a place, yet had never felt so cold, and I hated every walking, breathing thing for being alive while Ronald and my brother weren't. I cried.

Days later I was home for Christmas, and they were burying Ronald in the graveyard. *What is happening to us?* I asked. I went to New Orleans that weekend. Charine and Nerissa, so many of us, piled into one car and parked near the river. We walked toward Bourbon Street and the crowds. As we stopped at an intersection, we heard a gunshot and the crowds surged like water, as if a large hand had dropped a stone in the middle of us all. I grabbed my sisters' hands and we ran with the panicked crowds, half carried by the mass of bodies. New Orleans police rode on horseback through the streets. The horses were large and red, the color of Mississippi mud, and they boiled toward us, prancing and kicking with menace. Another shot sounded, and we scattered, our grip on each other so tight it was painful, and I wondered at us, running through the streets. *Running away from what?* I thought. *From what?* We didn't go home, and the crowds didn't disperse. We circled the block and fought our way back to the few open bars. I drank more through the night, drank until I would not remember what I did the next day, blacked out, and peed in alleyways like the homeless people I saw in New York.

YEARS AFTER RONALD'S death, I learned that his girlfriend did love him, although the night of his death she was too frustrated with him to say so. She was a curvy pale girl with brownish blond hair and light eyes. She'd been adopted and lived out in DeLisle north of the interstate. They'd gotten into a bad fight during the weeks before he died, and she'd felt threatened; at the time he died, she was attempting to distance herself from him. She was trying to avoid his phone calls, and when she did pick up the phone and talk to him, the conversation was strained.

"He called me," she said. Charine and I were in her car in our mother's driveway. Her car was green, and so wide across that all of us were sitting in the front seat. We were high. Charine nodded and I stared at the numbers on the digital clock, which were neon blue. It was 3:00 A.M.

"He told me he loved me."

The numbers glowed so brightly they seemed fuzzy at the edges.

"He said it right before he got off the phone. He said: 'I love you.'"

The minute changed.

"And I didn't say it back to him. I didn't. I was mad at him."

I bumped Charine's arm with mine, just so I could feel her next to me.

"But I did love him."

Charine chewed her gum, looked down at our arms.

"I did."

Later that night, after she'd left and Charine and I had gone inside to escape the sunrise, Charine told me she often had this conversation with his girlfriend. She said the first time his girlfriend had told the story about what happened before his death, the story about their last conversation, she'd cried. She sobbed at the end of that story, her voice breaking. *But I did love him, Charine*, she'd said. *I did love him. I did I did I did I did.* She'd said it over and over again, as if Charine doubted her, as if Charine were someone she had to convince, when Charine knew all too well the regret that comes with a lover's death, the regret that says: *You failed him.*

We all think we could have done something to save them. Something to pull them from death's maw, to have said: *I love you. You are mine.* We dream of speaking when we lack the gift of oratory, when we lack the vision to see the stage, the lights, the audience, the endless rigging and ropes and set pieces behind us, manipulated by many hands. Ronald saw it all, and it buried him.

WE ARE LEARNING
1991–1995

I prayed. At night, as the house clicked and ticked around us, I prayed that we would move back to DeLisle. I didn't want to be afraid to go outside, to be afraid of Thomas, who lurked, to fear what he would see in me and call me, to dread the hole in the woods. My mother heard me. After living in the seedy subdivision where every year the houses seemed smaller and shabbier, crumbling at the corners, ringed by weeds, we left Gulfport. After my mother cleared her narrow bit of land in DeLisle, she set a single-wide trailer on it. The property was on the top of a hill, surrounded on three sides by pines dense with undergrowth, and when we walked out of the front door, we only saw one neighbor's house. My mother aligned the trailer lengthwise on the property, which meant the left side of the trailer sat atop the hill, on the ground, and the right side of the trailer was elevated, supported on cement bricks, leaving enough room to drag chairs under and sit between the cement pillars. In the evening, little lean brown rabbits fed on the patchy grass that announced the interruption of the yard from the surrounding woods. In the evening, bats fluttered through the narrow gap in the trees above our heads, feeding on the mosquitoes that swarmed there, mosquitoes that bred in a hidden, shallow pond, dry during the winter, tucked away in the pine woods to the near west of our house. We were home, in our community again.

When we moved to DeLisle, my father moved to New Orleans. He thought there would be more job opportunities there, and he wanted to live closer to his brothers. After leaving us in Gulfport, my father lived with his teenage love, then moved out and lived in one small, dark apartment after another, of which there were plenty along the coast, sometimes with roommates, sometimes without. He stopped paying his child support and moved from job to job so quickly there was no way for the authorities to garnish his wages. In New Orleans, he lived in the small yellow ghost-haunted house with barred windows, where the wind echoed through the industrial yard behind it at night, bidding the metal to speak. Then he moved to a small two-story apartment complex with only six one- or two-bedroom apartments. The rent was cheaper there. The building was gray wood and red brick, and my father's oldest brother, Dwight, lived on the first floor. We would spend our weekend and summer visits there when I was in high school.

I'D BEEN THE only Black girl in the private Episcopalian elementary school during my sixth-grade year, and on my first day at the corresponding high school, I learned that this would be the case for high school, too. What I didn't know is that I would remain the only Black girl in the school for five years: in my senior year, another Black girl enrolled, but we never spoke. The one other Black kid in the school when I was a

seventh grader was a senior, and he acknowledged me sometimes with a nod, but most often ignored me. He was comfortable with the boys in the school, would hang out with
them in the hallways looking like a clone of them: polo shirts,
khaki shorts, slide-on boat shoes. I heard rumors that they
snuck him into the local yacht club to sail with them, because
he was unofficially not allowed because he was half Black,
which meant that according to the yacht club he was Black.
Today, I understand class also complicated my developing a
relationship with either of them: both of these Black students
came from two-parent, solidly upper-middle- or middle-
class families. They lived in exclusive neighborhoods with
pools and gyms and golf clubs and yearly homeowners' as-
sociation fees, and that culture was totally alien to my own,
one of government assistance and poverty and broken homes.
We had nothing to talk about. Most of the other Black boys
who enrolled in the school later, when I was in ninth grade
and until I graduated, were basketball recruits. They all
came from backgrounds that were closer to mine, and our
relationships were easier. I joked with them in the hallways
between classes whenever I had the chance, and during those
years those moments of camaraderie gave me some respite,
some illusion of community. But it was an illusion: because
of my distaste for team sports and my love of books, I was
still an outsider. I had friends, friends who were outsiders
like me in different ways: kids that were artists or writers or
loved pottery or punk music or theater, but they were never
my color. Overall, there were never more than eight Black
students in the school at one time. During my time there,

there were only three other students of color: there was one Chinese American girl, and later two Hispanic students, all three of whom came from moneyed families. At its largest, the high school contained no more than 180 students, and at its smallest, no fewer than 100.

Most of the students who attended the school were middle- to upper-class. Even though the school was flush with moneyed students, this was not reflected in the buildings. While the private elementary Episcopalian school I'd attended as a scholarship student in sixth grade was in a building much like the public schools I attended, redbrick with open airy rooms, the corresponding Episcopalian high school was nothing like this. Before 1969, the board of directors had purchased a mansion on the beach in Pass Christian to house the school, but Hurricane Camille hit and swept away the building. So the board built a big warehouse further north in Pass Christian, divided it into classrooms using thin walls and partitions, installed lockers in the hallways, and eventually built another, taller warehouse behind the school with spray-on yellow insulation that resembled dried snot. It was disconcerting to walk into the building, as industrial as it looked from the outside, and see all the students, who bore all the hallmarks of wealth and good health: braces, shiny thick hair, tans, and collared shirts. Some of the students were so rich they drove luxury cars especially tailored to their whims: Lexuses and BMWs outfitted for racing. Some of them slept on plantation-era beds that required small ladders to ascend at night. None of them lived in trailers. And throughout my school years, my mother cleaned for them. Sometimes she brought home huge garbage bags of their hand-me-down clothes after cleaning their houses. Joshua, Nerissa, and Charine refused their castoffs. I sifted through them, picking out what would fit, what I thought was reasonably fashionable, and prayed that when I wore it to school, whoever had owned it first would not see me in it. I assembled a ragtag wardrobe gleaned from my schoolmates in the hope that when worn together, my clothes would function as a camouflage, would allow me to be one of the group. I joined their religious youth groups too, became adept in the lexicon of organized religion, all in the hopes of being considered a little less of a perpetual other. But for some students, I could not escape our differences.

One day, a few months into my seventh-grade year, I walked into the gym and sat at the top of a small cluster of my classmates in the bleachers. There were four girls, all sitting with their knees together, all wearing khaki shorts and loose pastel shirts. I watched the other kids playing dodgeball on the court, hurling balls, intending to hurt. Barbara was idly twisting her blond hair: her roots were black. She turned in her seat to look at me.

"Why don't you put some nigger braids in my hair?"

"Excuse me?" I said. "What did you say?"

"Nigger braids. Why don't you put my hair in nigger braids?"

I hadn't misheard her. Barbara smiled, satisfied as an animal that's eaten its fill, and turned back to watch the games on the court. The heat in the gym was unbearable. I stood up and descended the bleachers, hoping I wouldn't trip. I couldn't believe she'd said the word, used it so casually, so denigratingly, and then been so proud of what she'd done. Casual racism was so prevalent in my school, yet encountering it often didn't make it any easier to understand. It was incomprehensible to me. I didn't know how to react to it. There were so many Black kids in public school that I could always rely on someone else to fight, to yell out *honky* and beat the shit out of the offending party. A few years later, my brother and his cohort would sneak knives and brass knuckles into school to fight White kids who wore rebel flag T-shirts, who initiated confrontations informed by race, by the word *nigger* hurled like a large rock. But at Coast Episcopal, I was alone. And the torments I'd suffered in Gulfport and public school continued, except at my private school, my brown skin was an actual physical indicator of my otherness. There was no need for me to justify my misery by imagining that others saw my sense of inner weakness, saw it as other, and picked on me for it; at my private school, the color of my skin was enough of a signal for some of my schoolmates to see inferiority, weakness.

I was alone later in the year when I stopped in the hallway during a break. A group of White boys, all juniors and seniors, stood in the foyer opposite me, loitering. They were uniformed in khaki and polos, and they were all at least a foot taller than I was. They were also laughing at a joke one of them must have told when I walked by. I stopped to look at them, me with my thin shins, unmuscled calves, a collarbone like a crowbar, my serious dusky face marked by a down-turned mouth that didn't like to smile since my protruding front teeth marked me as different in yet another way. My mother could not afford braces for me.

"What did you say?" I asked them. They chuckled.

"You heard," one of them said. His name was Phillip, and my mother cleaned for his family once a month. They always sent us the largest garbage bags of clothing.

"No, I didn't."

"You know what we do to your kind," another laughed.

"No, I don't."

They laughed again, each of them elbowing the other, and then I knew. Whatever the joke, it involved a Black person, hands bound, and a choking rope at the neck, a picnic. Lynching. They were joking about lynching.

"You ain't going to do shit to me," I said. I said it before I could think that I was one and they were many, and there was no one to help me fight my battle.

Phillip and his friends changed then. They shifted and stopped laughing. One of them crossed his arms, and then another, and they looked as if they could move like a herd.

Even though my heart felt as if it would beat its way out of my chest, I stood. I was sweating and my face burned, but I stood.

"You ain't going to do nothing," I said.

They saw I would not move. They watched my eyes, perhaps wanting me to cry. I didn't. The moment passed. They shrugged, walked past me down to the senior lockers. I watched them go. After they disappeared, I watched my classmates in the student lounge, sliding drinks across the table to one another, eating pizza, chewing and talking. I felt victorious for one moment, proud that I'd stood up for myself. But as I watched my schoolmates, their shining faces and white, wide smiles, separated by the glass between us, I realized I'd achieved nothing. I was still myself. I was still alone.

MY MOTHER DROVE us to visit our father in New Orleans on weekends in her small, rattling Toyota Corolla. Charine invariably sat in the front seat while the rest of us sat in the back. Sometimes we sang along to the radio, and when we did, my mother told us to shut up and let the radio sing. She had no patience, and I imagine it was because she drove and her children sang and all she could think about was our father and the fact that she had never wanted to be a mother in this situation. By this time Joshua was taller than me by at least two inches, and wider. Nerissa was a premature beauty. Charine was small, skinny, and funny. In the backseat, Josh and I would tussle with our elbows, each of us fighting for room by leaning forward and smashing the other person's arm into the seat. I usually lost because he was bigger and stronger than me; at the time, I was beginning to realize that all the dominance I'd exercised over him while we were growing up was fading. The trunk was even more crowded with paper bags filled with groceries; even when we weren't with her, my mother took responsibility for feeding us. She knew my father's refrigerator held only condiments. She packed easy things to cook, things she thought we could handle: Top Ramen noodles, tuna fish, eggs, boxes of Tuna Helper, sandwich bread, peanut butter and jelly, cereal, and gallons of milk. During the summer, when we stayed with my father for a week at time, we'd run through the food, so at the end we were eating dry cereal out of the box for breakfast and lunch, and inventing things for dinner.

"I'm hungry," Nerissa said.

"Are you hungry too?" I asked Charine.

Charine nodded, hopping in front of a large mirror my father'd set against a wall in the living room. She was preening. My father, as usual, wasn't home. He wasn't next door at his fourth baby mama's apartment, either. We didn't know where he'd gone. He did that often, leaving us alone in the apartment while he disappeared. I worried about him, but I knew that eventually, sometime later that night, he'd be back. I was accustomed to being in charge when my mother was gone or working, so I took it as my obligation. Of course I had to feed us.

Joshua took a pan out. We'd never cooked together before, but I needed help. I had no idea what to do with what little we had left over from the week. I opened a can of tuna, dumped it in.

"What else we're going to put in it?" I asked Joshua.

"Cheese," he said.

I dumped leftover rice from some red beans and rice Mama'd packed for us, and Joshua added some peas. Finally I added more cheese. It bubbled.

"What should we call it?" Josh asked.

"It looks like throw-up," Nerissa said.

Josh tasted a spoonful, then added salt.

"It's good," he said.

"Regurgitation," I said. "We'll call it regurgitation. We're chefs!"

We ate most of it. When my father came home, there was

only a little left. He tasted it, but much of what we'd saved for him stayed in the pot. Later on, he played music on the big stereo in the living room, and all of us danced in front of the mirror.

The next afternoon and evening, my father was gone again. My little sisters were at my father's baby mama's apartment, so our sixteen-year-old cousin Marcus decided he would take Joshua and me to the movies to see *Boomerang*. Five minutes into the movie, an usher bent over our seats.

"Joshua and Mimi?" *We're too young to be in here,* I thought. *They're kicking us out.* "Your cousin passed out in the bathroom. We think he's drunk."

We followed the usher to the bathroom and saw Marcus facedown on the tile. He'd been drinking before we got on the bus that took us to the Galleria to see the movie, but I hadn't realized he'd been that drunk. I panicked. Our father didn't have a house phone, and I didn't know the numbers for my father's brothers or his baby mama. We were marooned.

"What are we going to do?" I said.

"Come on," Josh said.

He walked to the pay phone in the hallway, began flipping through the phone book.

"Uncle Dwight's number is probably in here," he said. I hadn't thought of that, and felt stupid for panicking when my brother, three years younger, was so calm. And practical. Joshua found the number, and I called our uncle. Thirty minutes or so later, our father arrived at the Galleria in a big old Cadillac with white leather seats. Daddy dragged Marcus out of the theater and dumped him in the backseat, and we followed. I asked Daddy whose car we were riding in.

"A friend's," he said. I assumed he'd borrowed the car from one of his girlfriends.

"Josh had the idea to call Uncle Dwight. I didn't know what to do," I said.

Joshua was disappointed. Our tastes in movies had changed from horror to Arnold Schwarzenegger action films and Eddie Murphy comedies. Our trip to view *Boomerang* would be the first time either of us had ever seen an Eddie Murphy film in a theater, and he had really looked forward to it. Even though I hadn't been the one to faint in a pool of vomit in the bathroom, I felt like I'd failed my brother in some way that evening. But he'd shown me that he could be level-headed and solid when I could not be.

"That was smart," my father said. "Common sense. What happened to you, Mimi?"

I didn't reply to my father. It was the first time that someone had told me that I lacked common sense, and it was an odd thing for me to hear, since I'd been praised for my intelligence my entire life. My father probably meant it as a joke, but I couldn't see it as one; instead, I added it to the long list of reasons that helped me to make sense of why he'd left us, and why he continued to leave us even when my mother brought us to visit.

ONE DAY, TOPHER, a boy two years older than me, walked into the classroom while my classmates and I were taking a history test. My teacher had stepped out of the room to make photocopies, and she'd already been gone for ten minutes when Topher wandered in the room. He smiled at the classroom in general: when he saw me, he stopped for a moment, his face frowned long. Then he smiled and sat on my desk. I looked up and he began telling nigger jokes.

"What do you call a nigger that . . . ?" He said. He was taller than me, wore a dirty blond crewcut, and had a narrow face. He answered himself.

"How many niggers does it take to . . . ?" he said. He looked down at my head, and I looked down at my desk. He answered himself.

"What does one nigger say to another nigger when . . . ?" he said. I told myself: *Don't cry. This asshole wants to see you cry, wants to see you freak out. Take your test. Just take your test.*

"A nigger, an oriental, and a Polish man walk into a bar . . . ," he said. He finished the joke, leaned back and laughed to the fluorescent-lit ceiling. I was hot, sweating. I wrote down a word or two of a sentence, held my pencil poised above my test as if I were on the verge of writing something profound, something worthy of an A. Topher was impatient.

"Come on, Mimi," he said. "I know you know some good honky jokes. Why don't you tell them to us?" I stared at him and thought of how good it would feel to lunge at him, to grab his throat, to sink my thumbs into the skin and muscle over his esophagus, to push and see him turning blue. To silence him the way he silenced me just by walking into the classroom, just by being White and blond and treating the world as if it were made for him to walk through it.

"Topher." My history teacher walked back into the class-room, her blond hair feathered and framing the egg of her face like a nest. "Get out of my classroom." She didn't ad-dress what he'd said, the jokes. She hadn't heard. I looked at my classmates, and they looked at their tests. None of them said a word.

Some of them were my friends, and they never took up for me, for Black people, when I was in the room. And ac-cording to what some of them told me in private conversa-tion, they didn't when I wasn't in the room, either. Perhaps they were just as shocked or uncomfortable. I didn't know. One day, one of my classmates, Sophia, who was moonfaced with straight brown hair, cornered me in the student lounge during our study break.

"I heard something," she said.

"What?"

"Well, we were all sitting in Ms. Day's classroom, and she left, and we started talking about stuff. We started talking about Black people and Molly said she could never kiss one, couldn't imagine it because their lips are so big. And then Wendy told us this story about how some Black people pulled into her driveway to turn around and her dad started yelling at them to get out. She said he called them scoobies. Scoo-bies, she said." Wendy was one of the few other ethnic girls in the school at the time: her family was Chinese American. At the time, this surprised me; I hadn't expected this from another person of color. Years later in college, I'd read an essay by Toni Morrison that posited that this was normal for newer immigrants to the United States: place oneself in opposition to Black people from the beginning so that the members of that ethnic group would not be aligned with Black people, the lowest of the low, but would instead be aligned with others who disdained us.

"Like Scooby Doo?" I said. "Like dogs?"

"Yeah," she said.

"And what did you say?"

"I didn't say anything," Sophia said.

Why are you telling me this? I wanted to ask her, but I didn't ask because I thought I understood from her face some of why she told me. She looked sorry and guilty, her eyebrows drawn together and the ends of her mouth turned down. For the first time I understood that some of my schoolmates felt guilty by complicity, felt bad for keeping their mouths shut, for going along with it. For not taking up for me when I called them my friends.

"Well, thanks," I said. I squirmed on the dark green bench, looked down at my hands on the table. I didn't know how to respond to Sophia. I never even imagined confronting Wendy.

Years later, I understood that what Sophia wanted when she told me that story was absolution. But I didn't understand that when she finished speaking, her upper body leaning forward expectantly over the table. At the time, what she told me didn't mean much to me. I assumed that, regardless of the friendship we shared, a lot of my White schoolmates were racist: some of them, I thought, just had the balls to come out and say it in front of me. I should have spoken to some of my teachers about how I felt, but I didn't think to do so at the time. Later, when I was an adult, I told one of my science teachers about what had happened to me and she said, "I wish you would have told me." But I couldn't. I was so depressed by the subtext I felt, so depressed I was silenced, because the message was always the same: *You're Black. You're less than White.* And then, at the heart of it: *You're less than human.*

Sometimes I wanted to leave that school. But how could I tell my mother that I didn't want to take advantage of the opportunity she was working herself ragged to provide for me? I broached the subject once, spurred by two of my friends, artists and writers, who were leaving my private school to attend private boarding schools in California. *You'd get a scholarship so easily,* they'd told me. They'd even invited me on a trip to visit them in school, and though I knew racism was everywhere and the dearth of Black faces at their boarding schools scared me, I wanted to apply, to leave Mississippi, to escape the narrative I encountered in my family, my community, and my school that I was worthless, a sense that was as ever present as the wet, cloying heat. "You can't leave," my mother said to me. "You have to help me with your siblings." When she said that, I felt all the weight of the South pressing down on me, and it was then that I resolved to leave the region for college, but to do it in a way that respected the sacrifices my mother made for me. I studied harder. I read more. How could I know then that this would be my life: yearning to leave the South and doing so again and again, but perpetually called back to home by a love so thick it choked me?

★ ★ ★

AT THE END of that school year, Joshua lived with my father in his apartment for the entire two months of summer vacation. He was thirteen. By then he was taller than my mother, and he wasn't cowed by her in the old ways that I'd been cowed, or in which my sisters were cowed. He was self-assured around her, brutally honest and funny, would say things to her about girls he liked or his friends that I or any of my sisters would never dare to say. He was a boy, and my mother loved him especially for it. But she knew the danger of being a Black man in the South, and she thought my father could teach my brother things, important things, about survival, things she assumed she could not teach him. Even though she could have taught him about what it meant to be strong, to work hard, to love unconditionally, to sacrifice for others, to stand, she sent him to my father.

I missed Joshua but didn't realize how much until my mother drove us girls over to my father's and I saw Josh, his hair, the texture of mine, cut short, sitting in the living room, where he slept on the sofa, in a T-shirt and boxers. Nerissa and Charine ran into my father's room and began arguing over what they would watch on television.

"I hate that damn VCR," Josh said, shrugging at an old VCR sporting a thin scrim of dust in the corner of the living room.

"Why?"

"There are roaches in it."

"Living in it?"

"Yeah."

"Little roaches?"

"No. Big cockroaches."

"Well, how you know they live in there?"

"Every night I'm laying up in here, trying to go to sleep, I hear them crawling around in there. Then they come out and they fly around the room."

"What? Roaches fly?" I was aghast. All the reading and studying I'd done had not told me this.

"Yes. They fly in circles around the room, over and over. Like helicopters. Like they're trying to bomb me."

I laughed, but I was horrified. Roaches really flew? And then I felt a start, and wondered what else my brother knew that I didn't, living in New Orleans with my father, expected to be a grown-up in many ways, accountable for himself because my father was so absent, womanizing or socializing. My brother must have been lonely there, accustomed to the confined chaos of living with four women. He must have been as happy to see us as we were to see him.

"They hide in the VCR during the day. And it don't even work." Joshua laughed. "I don't know why Daddy's keeping it."

I'm sure my father looked at the VCR, like he looked at most broken things, and thought it could be fixed. He remembered the sixties and seventies, when the Black Panthers fed him and his sisters school lunches: he remembered how embattled Oakland had seemed at the time, and how it was able to come together under the leadership of the Panthers. He listened to Public Enemy and only Public Enemy. He owned all their albums. When we walked across the levee to the neighborhood on the other side, he talked to everyone, people sitting on the front steps outside their shotguns or on their narrow porches, walking in the middle of the street. He believed in the power of community, in the power of conscious political thought to fight racism and transform people who were browbeaten into those who had agency.

Whenever my father had extra change from whatever factory or security job he'd found, he'd walk us over the levee to one of the corner stores there, where he'd treat us to pickled pig's lips and potato chips and cold drinks. One day an older woman walked up to him, wearing white, her skin dark against the fabric, her hair pulled back into a ponytail. It was hard for me to figure out that she was a woman: she was so skinny she had none of the curves I associated with all of the older women in my family. Her forearms were the same size as her upper arms. She smiled at my father, and I saw that she was missing teeth, and those that were left were black at the gum line. And she was not alone. I looked at most of the people walking the street and saw that half the neighborhood looked as if they were starving. On our way back from the store, I asked my father about it. The sun was setting, and the New Orleans sky was pink through the power lines, which were tangled even here, where the parades did not venture, with Mardi Gras beads.

"Why is everybody so skinny?" I asked.

My father looked at me. He always talked to me like an adult.

"They're on crack," he said. "They're all crackheads."

Josh walked on his other side, munching on a pig's lip.

"All of them?" I said.

"All the ones you see that are skinny like that."

I frowned. The majority of the neighborhood was smoking crack. Skeletal men and women walked with jarring steps every day in an endless roam, it seemed; the only other people in the streets were one or two handsome teenage boys, a few years older than me, wearing wifebeaters and gold. They slouched on metal fences in the shade of spindly oaks, yet they still turned brown in the sun, and the walking dead clustered around them, while kids on bikes and on foot cut through the throng, playing and laughing.

But I wondered if my father's philosophies could ever make any sort of difference in New Orleans. My father's revelation about addicts and dealers made me see the neighborhood clearly, see the way the narrow streets were all pothole-ridden and mostly empty, where families seemed empty of everyone but the very old and the very young, the old driven to infirmity by crack, the young either ignorant or profiting from it. The air was redolent with the scent of marsh mud, burnt coffee, and something that smelled like raw sewage, but I sensed something else: violence driven by desperation and despair. Crack, with its low prices and quick, searing high, was eating away at the soul of neighborhoods and communities all over the United States in the late eighties and early nineties, its consumption driven by those desperate for escape, release. I was scared to walk through the neighborhood, and never did so without my father and my siblings. Joshua, however, was braver, perhaps because he had to be. He would have recognized the danger in that place long before I did, and would have known that he could do nothing but navigate it without flinching, smartly, or else be unable to walk down the street as a man. To be a man was to posture strength and capability; for my brother, this meant he had to be unafraid. He had to show a strength he may not have felt, had to evince a ruthlessness in his swagger that was not in him. The next weekend, when my mother brought us girls back, my father told me that my brother had been walking to the store during the week and two kids on a bike had ridden by and punched him in the back of the head. "Because he wasn't from their hood," my father said they told him.

"What did you do to them?" I asked.

"I talked to them," my father said, "and told them it was wrong." This approach, coming from my black-belt martial-artist father, disappointed me, but I didn't understand that this was exactly what his martial arts training had taught him. Violence should be the last resort. The music my father listened to reinforced that; there were other ways to resolve conflict. And in handling the situation the way he did, my father was trying to teach my brother to avoid the violence that plagued the Black community he lived in. Perhaps he thought he could raise a different young man, one resolute against the deluge of racism and socioeconomic inequality and history, and the self-loathing and destructive behavior that engendered. Maybe he wanted a son who could foment change like a Panther. At the time, I didn't see this, and all I knew was that I wanted to find the boys who had hit Joshua and fight them. I wanted to take up for my brother in the way I almost never took up for myself at school. *He doesn't need your hood,* I would have told them. When I saw Josh, he told me that the roaches were still on patrol, and he was still terrified of them. He made me laugh. Even though we were living in different households, we were still as close as ever. I wanted him to tell me about the boys, the bike, the blow, hoped that he would come to me the way a little brother would to an older sister. And even though we talked about mostly everything, he never did. He knew there was nothing I could do for him.

AT THE END of our last weekend of the summer, we returned to Mississippi and the beginning of another school year. On occasion, if my mother was not yet done with her duties for the day, she would pick me up at the end of the school day before returning with me in tow, while Josh watched Nerissa and Charine at home. The family my mother worked for lived in a large old mansion on the beach, which was painted dark blue and had a two-story guest cottage that had been ser-vants' quarters in the near past. On days like these, I sat off the kitchen with the wife, and as the children of the family, who were several years younger than me, watched television, we talked. I watched my mother clean; she was such a formi-dable presence at home that I couldn't stop looking at her, and this meant I had trouble paying attention to the wife. Why was my mother so silent? Why did she seem so meek? I'd never seen any of that in her. My attention was split between two worlds.

"What language are you taking in school?" the wife asked. She was tall and healthy and blond, robust and gregarious.

"French," I said. I watched my mother shoo the cat from the counter and spray the tile with Lysol before wiping it down.

"It's a hard language to learn."

I nodded. My mother rinsed dishes, began loading the dishwasher.

"It's difficult to hear the words, to tell where one ends and the next starts."

I nodded again. My hands felt wrong in my lap. I felt I should be at the counter, helping my mother, handing her dishes.

"Spanish is much easier," the wife said.

My mother bent, poured powder into the dishwasher. When she closed the machine's door and stood, she straightened like it hurt her. My mother grabbed a broom and began sweeping.

"Well, our family used to speak French," I said. "Creole French. So that's why I want to learn it." My voice sounded strange. My mother continued to sweep the kitchen, worked her way around the counter. The entire house had wooden floors, upstairs and down, and my mother cleaned all of them by hand.

"The best way to learn is to travel. Immerse yourself," the wife said. The family's parrot, which was as large as their cat and kept in a four-foot-high cage in a corner of the sitting room, squawked and spread its wings. Birdseed littered the floor. My mother patiently worked her way around the cage and continued sweeping. The parrot stretched its wings wide again, raising its beak to the air, stretching as if it would fly, but it settled. My mother pushed and the broom shushed its way around the cage. I nodded.

Years later, in college, I would encounter W. E. B. Du Bois and the term *double consciousness*. When I read it, I thought about sitting in my mother's employer's family room, watching my mother clean while I waited for her to finish so we could go home. I thought of how it felt to witness my mother at work, of how I saw her in a broader context, as a Black cleaning woman, almost cowed, and of how I was very conscious in that moment of my dark skin, my overbite, my irascible hair, the way my hands itched to help my mother. How my legs tingled as I sat and looked at my mother as she worked, and how I was aware that the wife was talking to me like an intellectual equal, engaging me, asking me about my college plans. How the privilege of my education, my eventual ascent into another class, was born in the inexorable push of my mother's hands. How unfair it all seemed.

WHEN MY FATHER moved back to Mississippi from New Orleans, my mother decided my brother should live with him full-time. My brother was still struggling in school, and my mother thought perhaps he'd do better with my father. My father moved into a long, low one-story redbrick house in Gulfport. The house was in a historically Black neighborhood, Turkey Creek, which was a community that had been established by freed slaves after the Civil War in 1866 and was still a mostly Black neighborhood of narrow streets, modest wooden-sided houses, and small, neat yards with immaculate grass, surrounded by woods on all sides. In some ways, it felt like DeLisle, except it was encircled by Gulfport's sprawling development. The creek they named the neighborhood after was notable mostly because it cut a large ditch and warranted a small bridge, and sometimes swelled when it rained. The woman my father'd had an affair with while he was living with us in the seedy subdivision had had a child for him by that time, so she and her child moved in, as did my brother. My brother wanted to live with my father, even though it was hard for him to change schools, make new friends, and leave DeLisle. When Joshua moved in with Daddy, he had his own room again, which he decorated with movies and kung fu weapons he took from my father, or things that he stole.

When Joshua was fourteen, he was a good thief. This was something that he'd never done when he was living with us, and it marked a new turn in him, one of the first that I saw in an ascent to manhood. To be a man meant one should be self-sufficient; he had to provide for himself. He was the same height as my father, and he'd lost his fat-boy belly, but the meat on his bones was evenly centered, proportioned in his long arms and legs, and would solidify to even leaner muscle. He wore big clothes that he didn't fill, and when he walked to the local Walmart with his new friends he'd met in the neighborhood, their large shirts and their oversize jean shorts were what they stuffed their booty in. They stole stupid things like boxers, candy, and Dickies pants, which he told me about when Nerissa, Charine, and I visited one weekend.

"I'm banned from Walmart," Josh said. I sat on his bed, which was made. His room was bare and neat. He'd been drawing pictures, and these he'd tacked to the wall, pictures of cars alongside pages ripped out of my father's lowrider magazines, which featured pretty Hispanic girls bending suggestively over elaborately painted Chevys.

"How you get banned from Walmart?" I said.

"We was stealing," he said.

"Josh!"

"It was just little stuff. Candy and boxers."

"What would have happened if they would've called the cops?"

"They didn't. They just took us back in the back and took all our names and told us that we was banned."

"You could've went to juvie."

"We done stole out there before and ain't got caught. The time before last they hollered at us when we walked out the door but we started running and they couldn't catch us."

I laughed at the image and felt like I was encouraging him, so I stopped. I'd meant to chastise him, be the big sister who reminded him of larger consequences. I was worried for him, worried at what the world demanded of him as a young man, and of what he would do to satisfy it, to stand. Yet I admired his recklessness at the same time. He was still struggling in junior high: then, I did not understand why he was having such a hard time in classes. He was smart, witty, adept at solving problems quickly and efficiently. Now, I assume he learned and tested differently from other kids, and the public school system didn't recognize that. Even though he stole stupid things from stores, he was still a tame kid: I knew he'd experimented with weed, but it wasn't something he smoked all the time. I also knew he'd gotten drunk for the first time with Aldon, and our older cousin had then loaded him and Aldon into the backseat of his Cutlass and spun donuts in the middle of the road, causing them to throw up all over his car. I'm assuming he was trying to teach them a lesson, and as far as I knew, it had worked, since Josh really didn't drink much after that.

"So I guess we can't walk over there and get something to eat, huh?"

"Naw," Josh said. He laughed. "Come on."

We left the house, which had the sort of low ceilings that feel oppressive even to me, a short person, and walked out into the street, where we stood for a minute before seeing one of his new friends, skinny and dark in the distance, his shadow trailing him like a tail, and we set off walking toward him. I missed my brother.

WHEN I WAS in school during the week, I wondered about Joshua, running through the hallways of a new school, being collared by new teachers, navigating the world without the luxury of having known all his classmates since elementary school. He was alone. Like me.

As I grew older, I became a part of my private school's community, sort of. I was a cheerleader and in the drama club, served in student government, and briefly revived the student literary magazine, but I was still *other*, racially and socioeconomically. My mother forbade me to date anyone (in or out of the school). Like most mothers in the Black South, she was terrified that I would become pregnant as a teenager. She didn't allow me to go to any of the school dances until my senior year, when I was allowed to attend my senior prom, alone. I hated all of the music. One or two of the White boys I attended school with were attracted to me, and I heard rumors that others were as well, but they wouldn't act on it because I was Black. They feared the judgment of their families and community. I found out how dangerous this intersection was when I was heavily petted by a boy one night during my senior year, and the next day, in conversation with another one of my classmates, another White boy, he said: *I don't believe in the mixing of the races.* Years later, I recalled that he'd touched me, but he'd refused to kiss my mouth or my face. My otherness was physically tangible. *At least,* I thought, *my brother doesn't have to deal with this in his school.*

To cope, I spent more and more of my free time, what little there was, at school, hiding out in the library, picking random books off the shelf to read. In seventh grade I read *Gone with the Wind*; while Scarlett's and Rhett's relationship spoke to the teenage romantic in me, the defeated Confederates' vilification of the freed slaves did not. And the fact that the book and movie were so beloved in America, across regions, horrified me. *Do they really think of Black people like this?* I wondered. My time at school seemed to attest that some did. By the time I was in my junior and senior years of high school, I was reading *Roots* and *Invisible Man* and *Native Son* and *The Color Purple* and, at my father's insistence, *The Autobiography of Malcolm X.* This was the early nineties, when conscious rap groups wore African-print clothing and Chuck D exhorted us to "fight the power." I wore a Malcolm X T-shirt that my father had given me to school and I was cornered by a girl in the bathroom and told: "Well, Mimi, I see I should have worn my David Duke T-shirt today." In my reading life, I was proud of my African heritage; at school, I was reticent. While I was reading and listening to Public Enemy, I understood resistance and fighting for civil rights as strength; when I was at school, I was bewildered. At home, I'd have moments of clarity while riding down the street with one of my friends, listening to Tupac, and I'd think: *I love being Black*; then a few hours later, I'd wrestle with my hair while obsessing over my antiseptic dating and social life at school, and loathe myself. When my mother picked me up from school one day, I began telling her about a school project, and she interrupted me, speaking to the pebbly asphalt road, the corridor of trees leading us home to our trailer, and said: "Stop talking like that." As in: *Why are you speaking so properly?* As in: *Why do you sound like those White kids you go to school with, that I clean up after?* As in: *Who are you?* I shut my mouth.

I worried about my brother. While I faced a kind of blatant, overt, individualized racism at my school that had everything to do with attending school with kids who were White, rich, and privileged in the American South, Joshua faced a different kind of racism, a systemic kind, the kind that made it hard for school administrators and teachers to see past his easygoing charm and lackluster grades and disdain for rigid learning to the person underneath. Why figure out what will motivate this kid to learn if, statistically, he's just another young Black male destined to drop out anyway? He was never referred to a counselor, never tested for a learning disorder, never given some sort of individual attention that might better equip him to navigate junior high school and high school. Both my brother and I were coming up against something larger than us, and both of us were flailing against it, looking for a seam, a knob, a doorway, an opening through. And both of us were failing.

★　★　★

I WAS SIXTEEN when I had my first drink. I spent the night with my best friend from my high school. She was a tall, generous girl who was unfailingly honest with me, who pulled me through some of my darkest bouts of teenage angst and adult depression, those times when my vision narrowed to a pinpoint and the world as I knew it beat me into hopelessness. We sat on the floor in her family's living room and took shots of cooking sherry. When the buzz hit me, I was euphoric. All the self-loathing, the weight of who I was and where I was in the world, fell away. I lay with her on the sofa, watching television, and said, "Mariah, I hope this feeling never ends."

"With as much as you drank, I don't think it's going to end anytime soon," she said.

We ran upstairs when her parents returned home. My euphoria turned to nausea, and I vomited all over her shag carpet. She cleaned up my vomit and helped me to the bathroom, where I spent the night with my face on her cool toilet seat, blacked out. The next day she dropped me off at my father's house, and I stood out in the road with Joshua.

I was cold. I wore one of my brother's jackets with my arms pulled into the sleeves to keep my hands warm, and I hugged myself. The skin at the sides of my mouth was dry, but my forehead and chin were dotted with acne. Joshua, who was fourteen, didn't have any acne. He wore a puffy Oakland Raiders coat, and he laughed as I told him about my night.

"And then I woke up on the toilet. I feel like shit."

Joshua smiled. He was winter pale, which meant he was a gold color, and his hair seemed darker than it would, sun-lightened, in the summer. He shoved his hands in his pockets.

"You smoked weed yet?"

"Naw." I wouldn't until I was eighteen.

"It's better. You don't have a hangover."

A woman was walking toward us. She wore a white long-sleeved long john shirt with black basketball shorts, and her calves were skinny and ashy. Her processed hair stuck up in sheaves over her head. I wondered why she wasn't cold.

"I liked it at the beginning," I said. "It was just when I wanted to throw up that things got bad. Ugh," I said, tasting the puke in my mouth. I'd vomited so violently it'd poured out of my nose.

The woman stopped and spoke to my brother.

"What's up?" She said this genially, with a grin. I thought maybe she thought he was handsome, as I did, even though he was at least ten years younger than her.

"Nothing," he said. "Just chilling."

They spoke as if they'd had this conversation before. I hugged myself, feeling a residual wave of nausea. My brother shook hands with the woman, and then she ambled away from us, one of her hands swinging loose, the hand she'd shook with my brother balled into a fist and held tightly to her chest, her hips swaying.

"She gotta be cold," I said.

Joshua looked down at me, smiled a small smile, so small I couldn't see his teeth. He let it go and shook his head.

"I'm selling crack," he said.

He looked anxious. He thought I would judge him, which I did, but not in the way he thought I would. The woman disappeared around the bend of the road, clutching what he'd sold her.

"How?" I asked. "Why? When did you start?" I shivered, hugged myself tighter. The fear that I'd felt for him grew larger, so great and immediate my back rounded in my brother's coat, my whole body tensing for a bone-breaking blow.

"I need money," he said. I didn't dispute him. Our father was struggling to make the mortgage payments on the house, working menial jobs that didn't pay well, first as a casino worker, then back to his adolescence as a gas station attendant. There was little extra money for food and clothes. Joshua was still too young to have a legitimate job. He may have been asking Joshua for money to help with bills; once, when my father was living in New Orleans, he'd asked me to help him pay his rent. I shouldn't have asked my brother why. My brother had learned: to be a man meant to provide.

"My friends out here," he said, "they do it. So one day . . . It's not hard—well, sometimes." He looked off in the distance after the woman when he said it.

"You ain't scared?" I asked him. He didn't answer.

I looked at the fine down over his top lip and his dark brown eyes and thought for the first time: *He knows something I don't.* Perhaps he'd looked into his own mirror and seen my father when I had only seen my father's absence. Perhaps my father taught my brother what it meant to be a Black man in the South too well: unsteady work, one dead-end job after another, institutions that systematically undervalue him as a worker, a citizen, a human being. My mother had found a way to create opportunity for me, to give me the kinds of educational and social advantages that both Joshua and I might have had access to if we weren't marked by poverty or race, so I was bent on college. Joshua had lesser models and lesser choices, and like many young men his age, he felt that school was not feasible for him. He never envisioned college for himself, a path through education to an upwardly mobile future, the American dream shining like some wishing star in the distance. For me there were hopes: a house of brick and wood, a dream job doing something demanding and worthwhile, a new, gleaming car that never ran out of gas. Joshua would hustle. He would do what he had to do to survive while I dreamed a future. My brother was already adept with facts. His world, his life: here and now. *Josh is older than me,* I thought. *More mature.* It was as if he'd drunk an entire case of Tabasco.

JOSHUA ADAM DEDEAUX
BORN: OCTOBER 27, 1980
DIED: OCTOBER 2, 2000

THIS IS WHERE the past and the future meet. This is after the pit bull attack, after my father left, and after my mother's heart broke. This is after the bullies in the hallway, after the nigger jokes, after my brother told me what he'd done as we stood out on the street. This is after my father had six more children with four different women, which meant he had ten children total. This is after my mother stopped working for one White family who lived in a mansion on the beach and began working for another White family who lived in a large house on the bayou. This is after I'd earned two degrees, a crippling case of homesickness, and a lukewarm boyfriend at Stanford. This is before Ronald, before C. J. This is before Demond, before Rog. This is where my two stories come together. This is the summer of the year 2000. This is the last summer that I will spend with my brother. This is the heart. This is. Every day, this is.

★ ★ ★

When I finished my master's coursework at Stanford in April 2000, I packed my things and shipped the detritus of my life via UPS to Mississippi. I was moving home. I wanted to live in southern Mississippi or somewhere near Mississippi in the South for a few years because I was tired of being away: I was tired of being small in the big world. I was tired of being perpetually lonely. During my senior year at Stanford, I'd sat in my college dorm room, a single with shag carpeting and a sink in a closet, and stared out into the courtyard at the moon, which shone brightly through the weave of oak trees. I ached so badly for my family and DeLisle that I'd cried. *How do I get back?* I'd worked hard in high school, spending weekend nights during my junior and senior years studying for standardized tests and navigating the unfamiliar lingo of college applications alone. Going to an elite college far from home hadn't molded me into an adult, made me confident and self-assured; instead, it had confused me, made me timid and unsure of myself. I yearned for the familiar. I wanted to live at home as an adult, independent but not far from the cradle of my family, my brother and sisters, my friends. My boyfriend at the time told me that he'd decided to take a job in New York after graduation, and even though we were five years into a relationship, I felt presumptuous following him to that city.

I packed the rest of my clothes in large suitcases and flew into the New Orleans airport, where my mother and nineteen-year-old brother picked me up in the large cream-colored Caprice that my mother'd bought for herself and then given to my brother for his first car. They loaded my luggage, straining at the seams, next to the speakers in the trunk. My brother played the music low, even though he had ridiculous beat. At our house, my sisters ran out to hug me. Nerissa was seventeen, while Charine was fourteen. They helped me unload my bags and bring them inside to the room I shared with Nerissa and De'Sean when I was home. Josh dropped my black suitcases on the floor with a grateful grunt.

I was home.

AT STANFORD, I'd longed for home and asked myself how to return, but I was shortsighted. I'd never asked myself how it would be to return. I hadn't thought about finding work, about how long I would stay in my mother's house, about what it would be like to return to Mississippi and feel mired, feel like I'd never left. To begin with, I couldn't find a job.

Both of my sisters were in school, and my mother still worked as a housekeeper, which meant that when I woke up each day to begin my tedious, demoralizing job search, I awoke to the silent house, barely cool in the heat, with my brother asleep in the next room. He'd endured only one school year with my father, coming back home when my father couldn't afford to pay his mortgage and moved into another apartment. The next summer he'd lived with my father again for a few months, but then come back to my mother's again. When he moved back for the last time, he told our mother, jokingly but not: "I'm never leaving you again."

Joshua and I awoke every day near noon, groggy and hot. He'd stumble out of his room, the smallest in the house, where his frame took up all of the double bed he slept in. He'd decorated his walls with art he'd done while he was still in school. He had a wall of VHS tapes on the bookshelf my mother'd installed for him. When my mother had upgraded to a double-wide four-bedroom trailer a few years earlier, she assigned Josh the smallest bedroom. He'd argued with her about it.

"You're never here," she'd said. He was always at work or spending time with his friends.

"If I had a bigger room, I'd be here more," he'd said. And then: "I'm the oldest now." Still, the smallest one was his, and, pressed by its confines, he sometimes left the house before I could ask where he was going. The sound of his car was louder than the sound of the day, the summer bugs buzzing in the trees, the electrical hum of the trailer like another larger bug: this is what woke me.

I went to friends' houses to use their computers to search for jobs. I filled out job application after application, printed out and mailed multiple resumes, but my English B.A. and my communication M.A. were virtually worthless in the southern coastal economy, which was ruled by casinos, factories, hospitals, and military bases. I began to apply to jobs farther away, in Alabama, in Louisiana, and after I realized I was failing, I extended my job search to Georgia and farther north, but had no idea about the challenges of being selected for a job when not in residence. Many of my Stanford classmates had been recruited by top consulting firms and investment banks, and my understanding of the job search was confused by the ease of their process. I called employers, pleaded for news, and my mother's long-distance phone bill grew.

My brother spent his days riding in his new car, an

eighties-model Cutlass he'd bought after he accidentally shot the gas tank of his Caprice while playing with a gun. He dropped off applications at gas stations, casinos, factories. He'd worked at a wax factory first, from which he brought home huge chunks of wax melted to look like amber. "It's beautiful," he said as he spun it before me. After that, he worked as a janitorial attendant at a large gas station, the first of its kind on the coast, that catered to truckers. It was directly off I-10, and he hated it. Part of his job included cleaning restrooms. He quit after working there for only a few months, but while he was there, he saved money and ate at the truckers' restaurant adjacent to the station, where they served cheap steaks and all cuts of meat thick with gravy. He liked the food, sometimes bringing plates home. While he may not have loved this low-wage work, he could still find beauty wherever he was; this was how he tried to understand the world, what gave his life some meaning, made his employment tolerable because the ugliness was clear to him, too.

"Why don't you like working there?" I asked him once.

"Truckers are fucking disgusting," he said.

It was June. Nerissa and Charine told us my mother had hinted she might kick Joshua and me out of her house if we didn't find jobs. Weeks later, Joshua found a job. The Grand Casino in Gulfport hired him as a valet parking attendant. He wore a purple shirt with the name of the casino and a little pot of gold coins embroidered in gold thread over his heart. He liked this job. He told my mother he was able to drive nice cars all evening and get paid for it. It was easy. My mother took the long-distance service off the phone because she said I was running it up too high, so I asked my brother to drive me to the gas station during his off hours, where I bought phone cards. None of it did any good. I remained jobless.

BEFORE JOSHUA FOUND the casino job, and in the periods between working at a fast-food place and the wax factory and at the gas station, he continued to occasionally sell crack to a few junkies in the neighborhood. This was his stopgap. It was a necessity for most young Black men I knew in the community to do so, at one time or another, to sell some kinds of drugs in a sluggish economy where their labor was easy to come by and totally and completely expendable. It was another cold day when I found this out, during December 1999, before the spring that I moved home. I was visiting from Stanford for the holidays. We were on St. Stephen's, and we were in a neighbor's front yard. Their house was old, dilapidated. Each piece of its siding was rotting, peeling away in gray and black and brown strips. The front steps were coming apart, nails surfacing like unshaved hair. The neighbor called Josh to the front door and he went, tall and pale, his puffy green and white Philadelphia Eagles jacket making him appear bigger around than he was. In the darkness of the house, the eagle dimmed to cream. He talked to her and she laughed: full and loud, throaty with a smoker's gravel. It threaded the air. She handed him money for what he gave her and hugged both of us before we left her and her friends to their talk, the dust-dark air, the clouded windows of the house. Later at our mother's house, I followed him into his room. It was warm, the Christmas lights my mother strung over the mantle in the living room shining rainbow bright under the crack of the door.

"You selling again?"

"Yeah." He glanced away from the television and toward me. Arnold Schwarzenegger was on the screen. "I'm looking for a job."

"For real?"

"You think I like to do this shit?" he said. "I ain't like the rest of these fools out here. You know when I got a job, I work."

I was his big sister: I was worried about him. He'd dropped out in ninth grade, enrolled in and attended Job Corps for a couple of months. After he was written up for not making it to school on time and threatened with expulsion, he'd quit. *Why'd you stop going to Job Corps?* I'd asked him. *Because when I drive to school in the morning, I got half-naked girls running out the projects and flagging my car down when they see it.* He'd shrugged. *What the hell am I supposed to do?* He wasn't kidding. Girls he dated actually did that, and I didn't doubt him when he said it; he was that handsome. Eventually he enrolled in GED classes. He'd thought about joining the military briefly, but after watching *Full Metal Jacket*, he'd decided that he was not a soldier. *I don't want to die like that*, he'd told me when I asked him why he'd changed his mind.

I knew then, dimly, how the world was changing, how America was hemorrhaging blue-collar jobs overseas, how factory jobs like the one my father had once supported a family on were becoming a rarity while only dead-end service jobs remained, and my brother was burning through those in search of something with a future.

"What you watching next?" I said, and sat on the edge of his bed. He made room for me, assessed his VHS collection.

"Don't know."

"Want to watch *Total Recall*?"

He shrugged, and I saw my father in him then, in the lovely lean globes of his muscled shoulders, in the straight, clean line of his collarbone, in the dimpled seat of his neck. He'd been husky so long it was a surprise to see him before me, suddenly a muscular, square-shouldered man.

"Okay," he said.

I settled in the dark to watch the movie with him, waiting for him to say something else, but he squinted at the television, and there was a line between his brows, his black-brown eyes serious. He rubbed the bottom of his foot on the carpet, and the smell that was him, that aroma of cut hay and coconut oil and salt, settled in the room. I drew my knees into my chest, set my chin on them, and watched Arnold fight the alien predator that threatened to kill him. He was outmatched and outmuscled. He was scrappy with brawn and foolish hope.

THERE WAS ONLY one time that summer that I felt like the big sister to his little brother. Most of the time I felt like the little sister, since Joshua had managed to find work and get his own car and tell me things that emphasized how naive I was about my life and his, repeatedly. I'd spent all the money I'd saved in college, around $3,000, to buy a used white Toyota Corolla in the summer of 2000. It was old and loud, and I was ashamed to drive it. *Shit, I'd drive it,* Joshua had said when I complained about the car. One day I called my father, asked him if he would change the oil in my car if I bought it and a filter, and he said yes, so I asked my brother if he would ride with me to the auto parts store because I had no idea which filter and how many quarts of oil to buy.

It was fall and chilly, so I cracked the windows, but it was warm enough that we rode without heat. Josh wore a dark blue plaid jacket, and he was large in my small car. Some of our friends from the hood, Rob and Pot and Duck, had given him the name Ojacc. *Because he looks like a big-ass lumberjack,* Pot said.

"Stop driving like a old woman," he said.

"What you talking about?" I said.

"You drive too slow."

"No I don't."

"And why you act like you scared to pull out?" He laughed, and I shrugged. I felt chastened, his little sister. "You can't drive."

We drove through the backwoods, evergreens tall at the sides of the road, the sky a pale blue strip above our heads, quiet houses here or there, the smell of the country in fall strong in the air: burning wood rich with the scent of pine needles and smoke. Josh lit a cigarette.

"You need to stop smoking," I said.

"I'm stressed out," he said. He'd seemed so much older than me for so long that I was surprised when he began talking about his girlfriend, who was living with us for a time because an older male relative had tried to sexually assault her.

"I love her," he said. "I don't know what to do. What do you do when you love someone this much? What about trust?" As a member of a community where trust—between children and fathers, between lovers, between the people and their country—was in short supply, my brother was struggling. Joshua drew in deep, blew the smoke out of the crack of the window; some of it butted against the glass and wove back into the car. She had cheated on him earlier in their relationship. He was asking me for advice. I tried my best.

"You just got to try," I said. "Forgive them. Trust them even though they did you wrong."

He shook his head.

"I don't know," he said.

"I mean, I think that's how it is. If you're meant to be together, it will work."

"I just love her so much," he said.

"I hear you," I said. It was the only thing I could think to say to let him know I took my designation seriously. "I hear you."

In the auto store, he led me to the oil and filters and then to the counter. After I paid, he grabbed the bags and carried them to the car. My head came to his shoulder. This was only the second or third time we'd been in the car together while I drove: we'd learned to drive at the same time, and since I'd never had a car before, while he'd acquired one early, he usually did all the driving. He was better at it, drove with one tattooed arm, the words *Sunshine* and *Scorpio* on it, resting on the sill, and the other, the words *Dedeaux* and *Ojacc* on it, at the wheel. At the exit from the auto store parking lot, I revved the engine, and in an effort to prove to him that I wasn't afraid to drive, I peeled out with speed. This was a mistake. The exit to the parking lot masked a large dip, and the car bounced down, the front bumper hitting the concrete and sounding a loud boom before bouncing back out. I swerved out into traffic.

"Oh shit," I said.

Joshua looked behind us. I expected to hear a dragging sound.

"I fucked my bumper up," I said. "I know it."

"It's probably all right," he said. Always level. Mature. One time I'd gotten mad at my mother, worked myself into a fury. Joshua had laughed at me. *Calm down,* he said. *Just calm down.* "We'll look at it at Daddy's house."

At my father's house in Gaston Point, we stood in a trio and assessed the damage.

"It's fine," Josh said.

"Naw, look at it," I said. "There's a gap between the bumper and the car body. That wasn't like that before."

"I don't see it," Josh said, his arms folded, his hip cocked to one side.

"You talking about right here?" my father asked. His long black hair was pulled back into a braid, which snaked down his back. He was in his early forties then, and his hair was still undiluted by gray, his physique still that of a young man, his skin still unmarked by wrinkles. I could tell he was proud that my brother was taller than he was, that he had grown into a serious young man, able to work on cars and provide for himself. "You sure that wasn't there?"

"It wasn't."

"You sure?" Josh asked.

"Yeah."

"Come on, son," my father said. He and Joshua leaned on the bumper in tandem, trying to push it back into the body of the car. Joshua slid his tall frame under the front of the car, pulled, grew warm in the weak autumn sun and had to un-zip his jacket. My father hauled him from under the car and helped him to stand. Joshua brushed his pants off and I went around to his back, swiping at the dirt and gravel and grass on his back and messy braids.

"It ain't doing nothing," my father said.

"It's alright," Josh said.

The car was already old and junky and now I done fucked up the grille, I thought. *So stupid.*

"You can hardly even see it," Josh said.

I breathed hard and imitated his stance, but folded my hands into my armpits for warmth. Josh was attempting to comfort me.

"You still want your oil changed?" my father asked. Years later, this ordinary memory gains heft, representative of all the ordinary days we shared, all the ordinary days we lost. It generates so much heat, it makes my fingers ache like a phan-tom limb as I imagine my brother alive and close enough to touch, how he would be warm on that cold day: the keloids of his scars, his scalp the color of butter.

MY FATHER CHANGED my oil because I couldn't afford to pay anyone else to do so. When my timing belt broke while I was riding to Pass Christian with my sisters and nephew in the car, one of my mother's brothers fixed it. My credit card debt climbed to over $5,000. I'd resorted to applying for a job at the local Barnes and Noble; they didn't hire me. I was desperate. When my former college roommate, Julie, told me she had a friend who worked at Random House, a book publisher in New York City, I asked her to send along my contact information and my resume and cover letter. My college boyfriend was living there, working in banking, and so was another close friend from college who was working for a record company. I knew a few people. If I was offered an interview, I'd make a four-day trip. If they hired me, I'd return to Mississippi, pack my bags, and move to New York City. If I had to, I'd leave.

JOSHUA AND I met in the hallway. This is my last real memory of him, and I hate it. I cannot remember the last time I actually saw him. I only remember this.

Joshua saw my suitcase on the floor in my room.

"Where you going?" he said.

"To New York to interview for a job," I said. I looked down and away and back to his face, tilting my head back. I wanted to say: *I'm coming back right after* or *I might not get the job anyway.*

"To stay?" he said.

I wanted to say: *It's just a visit.* "Yes," I said.

His face fell. I have read that expression in books before, and it is true: his expression slid from his forehead over his beautiful eyelashes, his brown eyes, to his mouth, where it settled in a frown. My brother did not want me to leave again, to lead. I frowned.

I felt I had no choice: I had graduated in March and it was now September, and I still had no job and had racked up debt. I charged a round-trip plane ticket to New York City and arranged to stay with my boyfriend while I was interviewing. My mother and grandmother took me to the airport, and as we stopped at the end of Hill Road, I sank down into the seat, feeling terrified and cornered.

"I forgot my ring," I said. My grandmother had gifted me a ring for my tenth birthday, which, on threat of never receiving another gift from her, she warned me against losing. It was gold and white sapphire, she told me, but later I found out the stone was glass. I'd worn it every day since I turned ten, and thirteen years later, in the back of that car, I didn't have it. "It's in the bathroom. I took it off before I took a shower. Please get it," I said.

"Okay," my mother said over her shoulder. She and my grandmother continued their conversation and I slid down in the backseat so my mother could not see my face in the rearview mirror as I cried silently, wiping my tears away with the backs of my hands. I didn't want her to see the irrational fear I felt at taking that trip to New York to interview; I wanted to appear brave and adventurous and smart, be the child she'd always wanted, the kind who took advantage of all the world offered, who journeyed forth from Mississippi with no remorse. I had no idea what I was doing.

★ ★ ★

WHEN I ARRIVED in New York City, I went directly to my college boyfriend's apartment, in a brownstone in Cobble Hill, an upper-middle-class neighborhood in Brooklyn. I was in NYC for four days for interviews, from October 1 to October 4, which I'd scheduled so that I could return home for Charine's fifteenth birthday on October 5. On October 3, I had an interview in the afternoon, with a placement agency in a high-rise somewhere in midtown. The woman who talked to me asked me questions and listened to my answers as if I were some sort of oddity. She smiled to herself at the South still evident in my voice, and perhaps wondered if that was going to be a problem with potential employers. When I exited the building, I looked up at the thin strip of sky between buildings, felt the city like a giant hand closing over me. I felt the energy of the place, the feel of limitless possibility and potential, but I was afraid. So many people, and how could I live without the sky? Without trees? I got lost on the subway, went uptown before realizing I had to head south through the Village to return to my boyfriend's apartment in Brooklyn, but I was proud of myself for eventually finding my way, alone, when my previous forays into public transportation had been limited to taking the bus from Stanford to San Francisco. In Brooklyn, I rounded the corner that led to my boyfriend's brownstone, which was on the edge of the neighborhood and next to a highway, and he was at the door. He was a banker, and he worked eighteen-hour days. What was he doing at his door?

"What are you doing here?"

He was tall, slim, movie-star handsome, which made

sense to me in some way since he was from L.A. He was from an upper-middle-class African American family, and while I'd been born red, he'd been born golden. His father was a doctor, and his mother's family had connections in Hollywood. He'd done all the popular, normal things in college: he'd joined a frat, been an RA, played intramural sports. What was not normal about his college experience was dating me. We came from such vastly divergent backgrounds. Every time some ill luck befell my family, some unique confluence of events that bespoke what it meant to be poor and Black and southern, it shocked him. He hadn't signed up for that. He wanted to be young and moneyed and have fun, and all the messy facts of my life, my history, who I was and where I came from, were anything but fun. He was the first real boyfriend I'd had, possessed of the same preternatural beauty my father had, and in the end he walked away just as my father had.

My boyfriend shook his head, didn't say anything, but his mouth was tight. He unlocked the front door and I followed him up the stairs, and he turned to me in the hallway and in a weird, slumped-over posture hugged me. He was breathing heavily. He let me go, and there were tears. Now his face was slack.

"You're scaring me," I said, but that wasn't true. I was nervous.

"You need to call your dad," he said.

"Why?"

He led me to the phone.

"Just call your dad."

I sat on his bed. Now I was afraid. I'd been sweating during the interview and I began to sweat again. The phone,
black and cordless, was slippery in my hands. My boyfriend
sat on the bed and watched me dial.

"Hello?"

"Hey, Daddy, it's Mimi."

"Hey, Mimi."

"What's going on?"

"I have something to tell you." He breathed, and the
breath broke. "Josh was in an accident last night."

"Is he okay?"

Again that broken breath.

"He didn't make it."

The phone came away from my ear and I leaned forward
and opened my mouth and sounded—I could call it a keen-
ing, a groan, a cry—something inside me, broken. My boyfriend's arms were around me but I leaned away from him,
thought I would vomit on his bed. *What am I doing here?* I
thought. *Why am I here and they are there? Where is my brother?
Where is he? But my daddy said, my daddy said, he just said he
didn't make it he's gone he's gone. He's dead. What? He's dead he's
dead he's dead.* And then: *My brother is dead.*

JOSHUA'D GONE TO work on the afternoon of October 2. He
hadn't been scheduled to work, but he went in anyhow to
pick up extra hours, to make a little extra money. He'd worked
his shift, parked expensive cars and not so expensive cars, left
his body's warmth and indent in their seats. Nerissa and

Charine drove to the casino to pick up Nerissa's check: she worked in a restaurant on the top floor of the casino's hotel. With check in hand, Nerissa and Charine stood near the main employee entrance, hoping to catch a glimpse of Joshua coming in to work. They'd seen him drive past the entrance of the casino in his gray-blue Cutlass, sitting high in his front seat, looking straight ahead, his face serious, his hair coming out of his messy braids, his profile sharp. They waited around fifteen minutes, and when he didn't walk through the entrance that was closest to the parking garage, Nerissa and Charine decided to leave, assuming Josh had walked into the casino through another entrance. That is the last memory they have of him. *I wish we would have stayed*, Nerissa says. *Five more minutes*, Charine says. We grasp at minutes, seconds, milliseconds. Years later, I would be grateful my family waited until October 3 to tell me Josh died: I'd had seventeen more hours wherein, for me, Joshua was still alive.

The night of October 2, he clocked out, and instead of driving up Highway 49 to take I-10 to the DeLisle exit, to home, he decided to take the beach road. I'd like to think it was a beautiful night, which is why he would have taken Highway 90 home. That the moon was full out over the Gulf, that it shone cool and silver in the clear sky, that the water glittered with its reflection. That the barrier islands were thin eyelashes on the dark horizon. That the air swooped down from the north and was unseasonably cool for October, so when Josh walked out of work and started his car, he rubbed his arms and said, *I love this shit*, loved the chill air on the down that wouldn't turn to beard on his cheeks, loved that he could look out of his window and see an open horizon over the water, where the waves from the Gulf quietly lapped the shore, where the oak trees in the median stood witness over centuries to wars, to men enslaving one another, to hurricanes, to Joshua riding along the Coast, blasting some rap, heavy bass, ignorant beats, lyrical poetry to the sky, to the antebellum mansions our mother cleaned and whose beauty we admired and hated. Eventually he split from Highway 90 and turned onto Scenic Drive, a silent, stately road set off from the highway by another median, by million-dollar real estate, when the drunk driver, a White man in his forties, sped up on my brother from behind in a white car he'd borrowed from a friend and hit Joshua's car at eighty miles per hour. Josh pressed his brakes by instinct, leaving black rubber smeared across the road, but there was so much momentum, so many bodies and cars and histories and pressures moving all at once, that my brother could not stop his car. He skidded sideways on to the front yard of one of those mansions. His car hit a fire hydrant, which came up through the floor, peeled back the metal like the lid of a sardine tin, and smashed into his chest. There was no mercy in this motion: the car plowed along, glancing off an oak tree before rolling and landing upside down on an immaculate lawn.

Joshua died.

AT MY BROTHER'S funeral, after the wake, after I walked up to the casket and glimpsed Joshua, who was powdery pale and awfully still (I thought: *This isn't my brother*), after I panicked at the lie of him lying dead, and after I sobbed through the service, hugging Charine, our skinny arms around each other, I walked to the podium and read a poem I'd written. I've since lost this poem, and I only wrote it because my mother asked me to, as part of the service. "I can't do it," I told her, "I can't write a poem." My mother asked me to pick out a picture for my funeral T-shirt, and I chose a picture of Josh and me when we were young, five and three, and we are sitting in the back of my father's black Riviera. I am looking seriously at the camera, and my brother is asleep on my small shoulder, his hair blond in the flash of the camera. We would have taken that photo around the time he and I sat on the front steps of the small, high, boxy house, me hugging him, bats flitting overhead, our parents arguing and breaking things inside. My mother asked me what I wanted my brother's funeral shirt to say, and I replied: "Nothing." I did not wear the shirt to the church ceremony, or afterward at the repast at my mother's house. I would wear it for the first time five years later, after Hurricane Katrina.

I can only remember one line from my elegy. Nothing about the line is original; I have since read it in other books. There is a common truth in its message, a hopeful refrain for those who remain. My voice broke when I read it to my family, to our friends, to the boys who would later lie in caskets, but who stood alive on that day in the back of the church.

He taught me love is stronger than death.

EIGHT MONTHS LATER, Nerissa called me. I'd been in New York City for five months then, and was living on a sofa in the West Village with wealthy friends I'd made in high school. It was 2001. Winter had broken, and tulips burst through grime-caked ground. It was the spring before the Twin Towers fell. I brought the phone with me into the small half bathroom off the living room, which was lined with ceramic tile. The girls who rented the apartment had begun taking Polaroids of their friends and taping them to the wall of the bathroom, so when I locked myself in it to privately speak with my sister, I had an audience, a sea of pale New York hipsters bearing the bored, poised, often beautiful faces of the rich. They looked at me.

"Mimi?"

"Yeah, I'm here."

"Mama and Grandmama went to court today. Mama said when they read the verdict, she started crying."

"What happened?"

"They sentenced the drunk driver who hit him to five years."

"What?"

"They didn't charge him with vehicular manslaughter. They charged him with something else. Leaving the scene of an accident."

"I don't understand."

"Mama said the judge called her and Grandmama in there afterward, told them why they couldn't charge him with manslaughter."

"But why?"

"Mama said all she could do was cry."

I began crying. All those faces on the wall were so still, so young. I hung up with Nerissa and called my college boyfriend and told him the verdict. I could hardly speak.

"What do you expect?" he said, impatient to return to work. "It's Mississippi."

All those eyes looked at me with such disdain. Here, a young woman with a perfectly symmetrical face and dark eyes, so beautiful it hurt to look at her. There, two boys shoulder to shoulder, each with one arm casually looped over the other's shoulders, sandy hair, pointy jaws. My conversation with my boyfriend was short, over after he'd asked, "What do you want from me?" and I'd replied, "I want a hug," and he'd said, "I have work to do," which meant no. When I hung up the phone, I sat on the floor and hid my face in my hands.

The man had been drunk. The police had found he'd been in several bars, and also been drinking in the casinos. He'd swerved at Ronald's sister, run her off the road, the night before he killed my brother. He'd hit Joshua from behind and had been going so fast that he'd swerved off Scenic Drive and his car had flown across two lanes of highway to land on the beach. That night, what had caused my brother's wreck had been a mystery. The police thought he'd simply lost control of the car, but the next day, someone called the Pass Christian police department and reported a car on the beach. The drunk driver had staggered home after he hit my brother. By the time the police tracked the car to the owner's house, it was the next day, and the driver was no longer drunk, and everything was cold. The drunk driver was in his forties and White. My brother was nineteen and Black. The man was arrested for and ultimately convicted of leaving the scene of an accident, which was a felony. He was sentenced to five years and ordered to pay my mother $14,252.27

in restitution. The man served three years and two months of his sentence before he was released, and he never paid my mother anything. Nerissa attended high school with his nephew, who attempted to apologize to her for his uncle. *He always fucking up,* she said he told her.

Five fucking years, I thought. *This is what my brother's life is worth in Mississippi. Five years.*

WE ARE HERE

In my search for words to tell this story, I found more statistics about what it means to be Black and poor in the
South. Thirty-eight percent of Mississippi's population is
Black. It is one of six states where African Americans consti-
tute at least a quarter of the population.[1] In 2009, the poverty
rate was greatest in the South, and in the South greatest in
Mississippi, where 23.1 percent of the population lived below
the poverty level.[2] In 2001, a report by the United States Cen-
sus Bureau indicated that Mississippi was the poorest state in
the country, in part because there has been little money ap-
portioned for rural development. The state has a median
household income of $34,473.[3] According to the American
Human Development Project, Mississippi ranks dead last in
the United States on the UN's Human Development Index,
a comparative measure of life expectancy, literacy, education,
and standard of living.[4] About 35 percent of Black Mississip-
pians live below the poverty level, compared with 11 percent

---

[1] http://newamericandimensions.com/drupal/content/10-notable-statistics
-Black-history-month.

[2] http://www.irp.wisc.edu/faqs/faq3.htm.

[3] http://www.census.gov.

[4] http://www.measureofamerica.org/maps/

of Whites, and "about one of every 12 Black Mississippi men in their 20s is an inmate in the Mississippi prison system."[5] Recently, researchers at Columbia University's Mailman School of Public Health found that poverty, lack of education, and poor social support contribute to as many deaths as heart attack, stroke, and lung cancer in the United States.[6] These are the numbers that bear fruit in reality.

By the numbers, by all the official records, here at the confluence of history, of racism, of poverty, and economic power, this is what our lives are worth: nothing.

WE INHERIT THESE things that breed despair and self-hatred, and tragedy multiplies. For years I carried the weight of that despair with me; it was heaviest right after Joshua died, when I lived and worked in New York City. In the morning I fought through crowds of people to get to the subway, to get a standing spot on the train, for my commute. I lived with rich White friends when I first arrived, slept on their antique sofa for five months, cleaned their apartment like a maid because I felt beholden, and walked their dog, which hated me. Next I moved in with my then-boyfriend, who charged me rent to sleep in the bed with him for the three months I stayed there. After that I moved in with an actor for nine months, and then with two girls I met through a friend.

---

[5] Matt Volz, "Male Prison Population Mostly Black," Associated Press, August 23, 2003.

[6] http://www.upi.com/Health_News/2011/06/18/Poor-education-deadly-as-a-heart-attack/UPI-89501308377487/?spt=hs&or=hn.

And as I moved from place to place, I was wandering around the city, bewildered and depressed as I tried to find the basics: Laundromat, grocery store, subway station. In the evenings, I commuted home in empty, rattling train cars and daydreamed or fell asleep, missing my stop and getting lost in dirty tiled mazes. I was hurrying past boys bleeding to death on sidewalks from neck stabbings outside movie theaters off Times Square. I was walking past homeless women with knotty dreads, women who held cardboard signs that read: AIDS HOMELESS PLEASE HELP. I was fainting on the F train. I was riding the subway at midnight to nightclubs with my friends, where I drank until I stumbled into taxis at four in the morning: deliriously, wretchedly, wonderfully, blackout drunk. I was buying liters of Brazilian rum and dumping tablespoons of sugar in glasses and topping with ice and drinking the rum straight, fancying myself a connoisseur of the caipirinha, three nights a week. I was smoking weed with Jamaicans until I was stupid.

And every day I was eyeing the tracks, the coming train, the third rail with its protective wooden shield, and wondering why I was alive and my brother was a year, two years dead. Each day I descended into the belly of the city, eyeing those tracks. And I thought about my family and how they would feel to lose me *and* Joshua, but they were so far away and my misery and grief and loneliness were so close. It slept with me. It walked with me down the crowded streets. I imagined my brother sometimes, when I was more lonely and desperate, imagined him walking to my right and slightly behind me, throwing an arm across my shoulders, and it would comfort me until I realized I was still alone and he was still dead, that he could not walk with me through those building-shadowed streets, through the garbage-stinking heat and the insidious icy snow, that he could not pull a coat over my head and protect me.

Sometimes I eyed my wrists, thought of how easy it would be to take a razor across the left one by wielding the blade with my right hand, and wondered if I could bleed out from just managing one cut. So I got a tattoo of my brother's signature on the inside of my left wrist so that it seemed like my brother had signed his name on me before he died, had made his mark across the cutting line. I did it because I knew that I could never make that fatal cut across Joshua's name. And when I fought through the crowds in Grand Central Station while trying to find a place to eat, a place where I could sit in a corner alone and disappear into the wall behind me, while I walked and fumbled past woman after man, felt all these people touching and crowding me while making me realize that I had never been so lonely, so alone, even though I was surrounded by young men in suits and older women in black woolen coats and sticky-faced children, I fantasized about cutting the right wrist with my left hand, so I got another tattoo in my brother's handwriting across the other cutting line on the inside of my right wrist. *Love brother* is how he signed the one letter he wrote me while I was in college. *Love brother* is what the tattoo says.

After I left New York, I found the adage about time healing all wounds to be false: grief doesn't fade. Grief scabs over like my scars and pulls into new, painful configurations as it knits. It hurts in new ways. We are never free from grief. We are never free from the feeling that we have failed. We are never free from self-loathing. We are never free from the feeling that something is wrong with us, not with the world that made this mess.

DEATH SPREADS, EATING away at the root of our community like a fungus. In 2008, a seventeen-year-old girl named Dariane attempted to cross the tracks in Pass Christian and was hit by a train. A few winters ago, Rog's sister Rhea died of septicemia from pneumonia, seven years after her brother died. A couple of years ago, a boy named Matt, who'd been like a younger brother to C. J., was shot; he crawled into the woods next to the road and died. Less than a year ago, a young woman named Shabree was stabbed to death by her boyfriend and left nude and bloody in the bed they shared; when relatives finally found their way to her house and her six-year-old let them in the door, she told them her mother was asleep and covered in ketchup. This is why I choose the option of a life insurance plan at every job I work. This is why I hate answering my phone. This is why fear roots through me when I think of my nephew, who is funny and even-shouldered and quiet, when I think of what waits for him in the world.

Yet I've returned home, to this place that birthed me and kills me at once. I've turned down more-lucrative jobs, with more potential for advancement, to move back to Mississippi. I wake up every morning hoping to have dreamed of my brother. I carry the weight of grief even as I struggle to live. I understand what it feels like to be under siege.

★   ★   ★

It is an awful weight. As the years pass, I find my memory shrinking and adhering to photos. I look at a picture of Joshua on his last birthday with a coconut cake bearing one burning candle and my brother a crooked smile, and I think: *I remember that day.* I look at another photo of him with his arm in the air, posing for me with all the other boys from the neighborhood in the middle of the street, and I remember the way he complained about my big camera and called me a tourist when I told them to stop for a picture on our walk down to the park. When I see him in profile, his eyes closed, wearing a red shirt, I think of the day I took the photo, how I had to look up to him to take it and the sun shone on him, blurred his edges, and I'd said to him: *Look at my brother! He's so cute. Just look at him!*

It is more awful when I see him in motion on old videotapes after not having seen him, except in dreams, for years. My mother found an old VHS tape and called me and Nerissa and Charine to watch it. She popped the video in the machine and sat back, her face impassive. I perched on the front of the bed, closest to the TV, and my sisters scooted behind me. On the screen, my brother walked through the living room of our old trailer, with its maroon carpet and cream walls, wearing light-colored jeans and a gray T-shirt. I had forgotten he was so tall. My nephew is one year old in the video, and he is wearing a diaper and nothing else. My sisters and I are in the corner of the frame. Charine presses play on a radio, and rap music sounds. My nephew throws his head back, bounces, tries to catch the beat. *Dance,* a voice says. *Dance, nephew.*

"Who is that?" Charine asked. "Who's talking?"

Come on, nephew. Dance.

I knew who it was. The voice sounded like mine, but deeper. Harder.

"It's Josh," Nerissa said.

I'd forgotten.

Do this, Josh says, and he is bouncing like my nephew, dancing. On the video, we laugh. I leaned forward, my eyes eating up my brother like a great hungry mouth, my body: a starved stomach. I would never be full. I rocked, sobbed.

Look at him, my brother says.

"I just miss him so much," I said. I could not help saying it: the words came out of me wet and ragged, and I could not stop for the hunger in me.

He's dancing, Josh says.

Behind me, my mother and sisters' faces were wet.

Dance, my brother says.

Every year on the day he died, I wake up to the dread of another year passing. I lock myself in my room, wherever I am living, and I cry until my eyes swell shut. And at the edge of the longing, the terror that I will forget who he was and forget our lives together immobilizes me, pulls me down further, until I am like someone in those cartoons from our youth, stuck in a quagmire of quicksand, mired in the cold, liquid crush, and then: drowning. After Joshua died, my father stopped working, lived on Top Ramen and hot dogs by working odd jobs, and watched television on two different sets at the same time for hours a day. My mother cleans my brother's grave every few weeks, picking stray grass, brushing the sand to an even smoothness. Every death anniversary, she takes to her room, closes her blinds, wraps herself in silence and darkness. Every year on his birthday, she buys mums for his grave and cleans the small ceramic figures of angels and teddy bears she's placed around it, while Nerissa and Charine attach balloons, one for every birthday year, this year thirty-three, to his headstone. "I only dream of him as a child," my mother says. "He's always my little boy."

This is grief.

BUT THIS GRIEF, for all its awful weight, insists that he matters. What we carry of Roger and Demond and C. J. and Ronald says that they matter. I have written only the nuggets of my friends' lives. This story is only a hint of what my brother's life was worth, more than the nineteen years he lived, more than the thirteen years he's been dead. It is worth more than I can say. And there's my dilemma, because all I can do in the end is say.

We were at McCloud State Park once, the only group of Black people there among a crowd of Whites. My aunt had arranged the trip to the park, and we sat in our own little segregated crowd in the shallows, me and Nerissa and Charine and Joshua, our cousins Rufus and Dornell, and a few other boys from the neighborhood, Duck and Hilton and Oscar and C. J., and we drank beer, tossing the brown and gold bottles back toward the shore, where we would collect them in a gar-bage bag. The day was hot, the beach small, Black and White studiously ignoring each other. There were high, fluffy clouds in the sky, and we swam in the amber-dark river, sat on the red clay dirt shore and brushed sand from our shoulders. When a white boat chugged up the river, flat and topless, with a gathering of men and one woman, all White and mottled red from the sun, feathered hair bleached in the light, the other White people on the bank cheered. A Confederate flag flew from a staff at the prow, and one of the men on the bank with us lifted his arms above his head, crossing them at mid-elbow so that they made an X, and howled. *He's making the bars,* I thought, and suddenly I wanted to leave these White people to their beach, their stars and bars, their glances, the howl that said what so many of the White politicians in Mississippi have said in coded language, one time or another: *You're nothing.*

Josh was standing near the front of his parked Cutlass, which was blue and dull in the heavy light. His girlfriend Tasha stood before him, small and pale. There hadn't been enough sun that day to tan. His hair snaked over his head and down his forehead, sandy and alive. He tossed his head back so that he could see us all clearly.

"I don't know what y'all looking so surprised for," he said. He addressed us all, but he looked at me when he said it. "White people got gangs just like us."

Joshua made sense of the world in his own way. Or at least he was trying to for the short time that he was here. He was attempting to see the patterns, to find the story behind the statistics that I would write about years later. He wanted meaning. There was an older Black man who set up shop with a card table and a folding chair outside the doors of the local supermarket in Pass Christian, a supermarket that would disappear after Hurricane Katrina, its steel beams bent to look like twisted, spindly trees. The man fashioned crosses from plastic and string, wove intricate designs into the crucifixes, and sold them. Sometimes at night, on one of his rides, Josh would stop and sit with the man, talk to him, ask him questions: *What do you know about God? Why are we here?* And the man, who had maybe sold one cross earlier in the night for a few dollars, happier at the fact it was bought than by the money it gave him, was pleased at having this tall young olive-skinned man sitting there with him asking him questions instead of swaggering by, pants low on his hips, wifebeater not quite meeting his shorts at the waist, flashing underwear, smelling of smoke and deodorant and salt; this older gentleman would have smiled and said—

I do not know what answers this Black man gave my brother, nor if they made sense to Joshua. Perhaps Josh thought about the churchman's answers when he stood at the edge of a crowd, his brindle pit bull on a tight leash, and watched the rest of us talking and laughing with each other in clusters in the street after the Easter Sunday ballgame. Perhaps he thought about the churchman's answers one winter night when we were at Hilton's house: Joshua, Duck, Nerissa, C. J., Rob, Aldon, Charine, Hilton, Dornell, Pot, Deandre, Tasha, and I. I was sitting in a chair at a table in the kitchen and holding a can of beer in my hand. A case of Budweiser sat before me, and we were all drinking. Hilton's mother was absent; she didn't care what we did, and she let us have the run of the house. She was somewhere out in that chilly night, a night so cold it seeped through the floorboards. I was so drunk that I could not sit upright in my chair. I slid down so that the back of the chair was at my neck and my head rested on it. I felt better that way. My brother walked in from the living room and stood before me with his beer. He was more sober than I, and often serious, drunk or sober.

"What are you doing?" he asked. I gulped down my beer.

I felt good, which didn't happen often; I was often unhappy, depressed and homesick. After my brother and my friends died, I would learn I'd known less of unhappiness than I thought. On that cold night, I was proud of myself because I was home for Christmas break and I was keeping up with my brother. I was happy we were hanging out. I was drinking as much as he was, and I was only five foot three and 110 pounds while he was six foot one and around 190 pounds, and I was not sick yet. I wanted him to know what I thought of him, that I loved him and admired him, that I wanted to grow up and be like him, so I opened my mouth and raised my can to him and said, "I'm rolling with the big dogs. I'm rolling with the big dogs!" in tribute. I was too drunk for eloquence. I was his sister. He looked at me, his eyes soft. I wonder if he thought about the fact he'd have to carry me to his car and slide me into the backseat, about the moment, which neither of us remembered, when he'd become the big brother, the protector, the one who walked through the door first, and I'd become his little sister.

"She's crazy," Tasha said.

"She's drunk," Joshua laughed.

Joshua would have thought about his questions, the answers the world had given him about his place in it, every time he walked into the room I shared with Nerissa while I was home from college for a few days, a week, a month, and during those six months I lived at home before he died. On those nights, he said: "Come take a ride with me."

I was a bitch to him often during the summer, snapping at

him and fighting with him over small things, like him not wanting to watch our nephew De'Sean while I was on baby-sitting duty, or him heating up buckets of chitterlings in the microwave so the stink pervaded the house, but I never told Josh no when he asked me to ride. We argued and forgot we argued. Each time he invited me to come along with him, I felt special that he'd asked, pleased that he wanted to spend time with me. After he died, I wonder if he'd known it. The last time we rode is the one I remember most clearly: he wore jean shorts and a wifebeater, and his hair was uncombed. I followed him out of the front door. It was night, and the air was wet and warm, and when we got into the car, the seats felt damp. When Josh cranked the car, it scratched and rum-bled to life, and we both rolled down the windows, manu-ally; the knobs were slick. Immediately his radio sounded. He played songs on the stereo for me that beat obscenely because his speakers were so loud. Years later, I can only remember one of the songs, and it was the last: Ghostface Killah's "All I Got Is You."

"I got something I want to play for you," Joshua said.

He turned up the music, blasted it. This is for all the fami-lies, Ghostface said. This is for yours, I heard. The trunk rat-tled. Thinking about the past, when he was young, Ghostface said. The bats spastically caught their dinners. They were poor, Ghostface said. Armadillos crept along ditches and froze in the headlights. His father left him at the age of six, and after his mother packed his father's shit and kicked him out, she cried, Ghostface said. The pines waved to the dark. The trees fell away like great waves. *Sometimes I look up at the*

stars and analyze the sky, and ask myself was I meant to be here . . .
why? Ghostface spat, like he could not wait to get it out of
him, could not bear keeping it inside any longer.

"This reminds me of us," Josh said.

We rode away from St. Stephen's, away from the house,
away from the cluster of houses of our Black neighborhood,
out into the White outskirts of DeLisle, toward the bayou
and over the bridges, the water shimmering silver in the
night, the grass black. My brother played the song over and
over again, and all that we'd been and become sat with us like
another sibling in the passenger seat. We rode through Pass
Christian, down to the beach, along Scenic Avenue, where
he would die months later, so we could see the Gulf stretching out over the horizon, the sands white as tombstones. I
looked away from Josh and out of the window so he couldn't
see my face, and I cried as we rode, thinking of our mother,
our father, Charine and Nerissa and him. I wiped my face
and was ashamed, but Josh didn't say anything. He drove us
away from the beach and back up through Pass Christian,
through the bayou, past St. Stephen's, and up into the country, away from all the houses, all the lights, so we rode alone
under the black bowl of the sky, the stars' fire so cold, so far
away. Here, a dark horse and a white horse fed on grass at the
side of the road, and when we passed them, they were dim
and ghostly, hardly there. Vines grew over the limbs of trees
and over the power lines, hung down into the street lamps,
so the leaves of the vines gleamed like Christmas lights. The
wind pushed our chests with a firm hand into the seats of the
car. We rode like we could drive far and long enough to out-

run our story, what Ghostface said: *To all the families that went through the struggle.* But in the end, we could not.

I don't ride with anyone like that anymore. When I hang out with my male cousins, with Rufus or Broderick or Donnie or Rhett or Aldon, or with my friend Mark, I do ask them to drive, but it's not the same. When we ride through the roads that cut through the forests of DeLisle, sometimes I close my eyes and take another drink and feel the wind again like a hand on my face, and I think about Joshua, and then the man who drives, who could be my brother, tall and solemn in the driver's seat, right hand looped casually over the steering wheel, becomes him, and for a moment my brother is there next to me, navigating, leading. And then the wind buffets my eyes open, and the trees shiver darkly at both sides of the road and the air smells of burning pine needles, and I open my eyes to what is.

When Joshua died, he took so many of our stories with him. My sisters are too young to remember them. They cannot see the full enormity of what happened because they did not live what we did. I write these words to find Joshua, to assert that what happened *happened*, in a vain attempt to find meaning. And in the end, I know little, some small facts: I love Joshua. He was here. He lived. Something vast and large took him, took all of my friends: Roger, Demond, C. J., and Ronald. Once, they lived. We tried to outpace the thing that chased us, that said: *You are nothing.* We tried to ignore it, but sometimes we caught ourselves repeating what history said, mumbling along, brainwashed: *I am nothing.* We drank too much, smoked too much, were abusive to ourselves, to each other. We were bewildered. There is a great darkness bearing down on our lives, and no one acknowledges it.

WE WHO STILL live do what we must. Life is a hurricane, and we board up to save what we can and bow low to the earth to crouch in that small space above the dirt where the wind will not reach. We honor anniversaries of deaths by cleaning graves and sitting next to them before fires, sharing food with those who will not eat again. We raise children and tell them other things about who they can be and what they are worth: to us, everything. We love each other fiercely, while we live and after we die. We survive; we are savages.

When I was twelve years old, I looked in the mirror and I saw what I perceived to be my faults and my mother's faults. These coalesced into a dark mark that I would carry through my life, a loathing of what I saw, which came from others' hatred of me, and all this fostered a hatred of myself. I thought being unwanted and abandoned and persecuted was the legacy of the poor southern Black woman. But as an adult, I see my mother's legacy anew. I see how all the burdens she bore, the burdens of her history and identity and of our country's history and identity, enabled her to manifest her greatest gifts. My mother had the courage to look at four hungry children and find a way to fill them. My mother had the strength to work her body to its breaking point to provide for herself and her children. My mother had the resilience to cobble together a family from the broken bits of another. And my mother's example teaches me other things: This is how a transplanted people survived a holocaust and slavery. This is how Black people in the South organized to vote under the shadow of terrorism and the noose. This is how human beings sleep and wake and fight and survive. In the end, this is how a mother teaches her daughter to have courage, to have strength, to be resilient, to open her eyes to what is, and to make something of it. As the eldest daughter of an eldest daughter, and having just borne a daughter, I hope to teach my child these lessons, to pass on my mother's gifts.

Without my mother's legacy, I would never have been able to look at this history of loss, this future where I will surely lose more, and write the narrative that remembers, write the narrative that says: *Hello. We are here. Listen.* It is not easy. I continue. Sometimes I am tireless. And sometimes I am weary. And when I am weary, I imagine this: After the moment I die, I will find myself standing on the side of a long, pitted asphalt road flanked on both sides by murmuring pine trees, under a hot, high sun in a blue sky. In the distance, I will hear a rumbling thumping, a bass beat. A dull blue '85 Cutlass will cut the horizon, come growling down the road before stopping in front of me. It will stop so quickly the gravel will crunch, and then my brother will swing the passenger door wide with one long tattooed arm, the other on the wheel. He will look at me with his large dark liquid eyes, his face soft. He will know that I have been waiting. He will say: *Come. Come take a ride with me.* I will, brother. I'm here.

ACKNOWLEDGMENTS

First, of course, I'd like to thank the families of the young men I've written about in this book, who were invaluable resources for me as I attempted to tell some of the stories of our loved ones' lives. I could not have written any of this without you sharing your love and grief with me, so my boundless gratitude goes to the immediate and extended families of Roger Daniels, Demond Cook, Charles Martin, and Ronald Dedeaux. Special gratitude goes to Dwynette, Rob, Cecil, and Selina, who patiently answered question after question about their cousins/loved ones.

I've been blessed with a most excellent writer's group: Sarah Frisch, Stephanie Soileau, Justin St. Germain, Mike McGriff, J. M. Tyree, Ammi Keller, Will Boast, Harriet Clark, Rob Ehle, Raymond McDaniels, and Elizabeth Staudt. Sarah Frisch was especially helpful, talking me through the book, chapter by chapter, when I was still unsure I'd even written a memoir. The wonderful faculty and students I worked with during my Stegner Fellowship at Stanford University also helped me immensely in this project, especially Tobias Wolff and Elizabeth Tallent. I wrote the first draft of this book while I was the Grisham Writer in Residence at the University of Mississippi, so I must thank everyone there and in the surrounding community of Oxford, Mississippi, who welcomed me into the fold of their literary community and made my time there productive, instructive, and rewarding, especially Ivo Kamp and Richard Howorth. I'd like to thank the University of Michigan for believing in me and teaching me and mentoring me, especially Peter Ho Davies, Laura Kasischke, Eileen Pollack, and Nicholas Delbanco. Special thanks to Thomas Lynch, who taught me so much about creative nonfiction and who was the first person to encourage me to write about my grief, which became the seed of this book in an essay I wrote for his class. He was unfailingly kind and encouraging and read the essay aloud when my voice failed me.

I'd like to thank my agent, Jennifer Lyons, for first suggesting that I had a memoir in me, and for believing and being passionate about my work from the very beginning. My publicist, Michelle Blankenship, for being an amazing publicist and an excellent friend who humors me when I am in New York City and feel like eating Korean BBQ for three hours. I'd like to thank my dear friend and editor, Kathy Belden, who saw this manuscript when it was half-realized and, with careful reading, brilliant feedback, and meticulous prodding, helped me to write the best book I could. I'd be a much worse writer without her.

My mother has been after me for two books to thank the man who provided me with a scholarship to my exceptional high school, so in my third, I'd like to thank Riley Stonecipher for seeing potential in me and generously offering to help me get a better education. The world is a better place with people like him in it, who give and help where help is needed. There were many friends, teachers, and librarians at my high school who saw potential in me and helped me become the writer I am: especially Mariah Herrin, Kristin Townson, and Nancy Wrightsman.

Finally I'd like to thank the hood in DeLisle, without which I could not have lived this to write it: Blue, Duck, Loc, C-Sam, Scutt, Pot, Fat Pat, Darrell, Darren, Jon-Jon, Ton-Loc, Tasha, Oscar, B. J., Marcus, L. C., Rem, and Moody-Boy (many of whom told me their stories and helped me write this book). I'd like to thank my friends and cousins who comforted me when writing was almost unbearable: Mark Dedeaux, Aldon Dedeaux, and Jillian Dedeaux. There were days where I could not write another word without you telling me: *It will be all right.* B. Miller for knowing exactly when I need to laugh so I won't cry. My father for telling me stories about our family, for stressing the importance of history and memory, and for teaching me to believe in community. My grandmother Dorothy for helping me learn the family's history, for teaching me how to be a strong, beautiful woman, and for cooking me special dishes. My mother for giving me permission to write this book, for clarifying facts about our family heritage, for mothering us when we wandered in the wild, and of course, for making a way out of no way every day. My niece, Kalani, and my nephew, De'Sean, for making me be silly when I need it and hugging me when I need it and giving me hope that tomorrow will have light. My baby, Noemie, for waking me everyday and reminding me to be grateful and amazed that we are here, for teaching me I can do what I previously thought impossible, and for making me happy to be alive. My sister Charine, who insisted that I write this book, who helped me research so much of it, and who pushed me to tell our story when I didn't want to. And finally my sister Nerissa, who saved my computer during Hurricane Katrina, and who was the first person to tell me that I must tell our story, the first to insist this story was worth reading. My sisters, I am forever in your debt. In closing, I'd like to thank every one of the aforementioned for loving me, for walking with me through this trial, and for giving me a home. Thank you.

A NOTE ON THE AUTHOR

JESMYN WARD grew up in DeLisle, Mississippi. She received her M.F.A. from the University of Michigan and has been a Stegner Fellow at Stanford and a Grisham Visiting Writer in Residence at the University of Mississippi. She is currently an assistant professor of creative writing at the University of South Alabama. She is the author of the novels *Where the Line Bleeds* and *Salvage the Bones*, for which she won the 2011 National Book Award and the Richard Wright Literary Excellence Award, and was a finalist for the New York Public Library Young Lions Literary Award and the Dayton Literary Peace Prize, as well as a nominee for the IMPAC Dublin Literary Award.